INSANE JEALOUSY

The causes,
outcomes,
and solutions
when jealousy
gets out of
hand.

THE TRIANGLE OF THE MIND

by
Vijai P. Sharma Ph. D.
"Ashley"
"Sabrina"
"Holly"

MIND PUBLICATIONS, CLEVELAND, TENNESSEE

4

INSANE JEALOUSY
The Causes, Outcomes, And Solutions When Jealousy
Gets Out Of Hand
The Triangle of the Mind

Vijai P. Sharma, Ph.D
"Sabrina," "Ashley," and "Holly"

Mind Publications, Cleveland
P.O. Box 4254
Cleveland, TN 37320-4254

Library of Congress Catalog Card Number 90-92291

ISBN O-9628382-6-8 $16.95 Softcover

Subject Index
Jealousy; Delusional Jealousy; Delusions; Paranoia;
Domestic Violence; Battering; Spouse Abuse; Marital
Discord; Marriage Counseling.
Bibliography
Includes index

Cover: William Blumhoff Design

ABOUT THE BOOK AND THE AUTHORS

"Sabrina" and "Ashley" are two sisters whose father suffered from a delusional disorder of jealousy. As a result of this disorder, he killed their mother and committed suicide. They have contributed the story, "Mother and Dad."

Holly was the wife of a morbidly jealous man who committed suicide out of his jealous rage and desperation. She has contributed the story, "My Husband."

Sabrina, Ashley, and Holly have borne the ultimate consequences of a jealousy disorder and are now putting their lives together and trying to help others who are in a similar situation. Although, in their stories, names, places, and other identifying details are disguised, they are aware that publication of their stories may lead to misunderstandings and cause emotional distress not only to them but their families as well. They are willing to take that risk in the hope that this book will help the individuals and their families afflicted by this least understood human problem.

Vijai P. Sharma, Ph.D, a clinical psychologist and counselor for Sabrina, Ashley, Holly, other victims, and patients of pathological jealousy, discusses the disorder and the management of jealousy. Dr. Sharma, clinical director of a community mental health center, and licensed as a clinical psychologist in Tennessee, has received extensive clinical training in India, England, and Sweden.

What the pilot readers are saying:

The author has identified a major problem in our society and has eloquently differentiated between what is normal jealousy and that of pathological jealousy with its potential hazards. I would urge every professional who is dealing with and treating patients in the area of mental health, as well as non-professional to read this book through from cover to cover. It is within itself a masterpiece.
Kenneth E. Shoemaker, M.D.

Outstanding book. Dr. Sharma has provided a wonderful tool for all of us to use. He and his co-writers are very courageous indeed.
Barry Kidwell, Pastor.

Dr. Sharma has created a masterpiece within the pages of this book. I became so absorbed in it that I read it completely through in one evening. It is enlightening and it ventures into new territories.
Suzan Logsdon, Executive Assistant.

Since I first reviewed the manuscript, I have had a case in my own private practice of a "delusionally jealous" woman. I sincerely believe that I would be able to use this book to help my college students live a more healthy and wholesome life. I also believe this knowledge will help me identify clients or their families who are trapped by this relentless disease.
Jacqueline H. Bailey , M.Ed., Ed.S.

The author deals with a subject that has too long been held in secret by American families. It is a honest, straight forward look at a problem which is destroying many homes today. The hurting people who were victims have put their total personal feelings on paper
Dr. Ronald V. Free, D.C.

Dr. Sharma's book on jealousy is opening our eyes to an often subdued suffering in relationships. A lot of readers will be able to recognize themselves in the mirror of his fellow authors' case studies.
William W. Van Groenou, Ph.D
Professor of Sociology.

WHAT IS INSANE JEALOUSY?

Insane jealousy is the fixed belief that one's partner is unfaithful and sexually cheating one behind his back. The belief of an insanely jealous person regarding the unfaithfulness of his partner is not founded in reality. Albeit, this belief is not changeable by objective reasoning or reasonable explanations. This belief is firmly entrenched and unshakeable. Any counter evidence, assertion of faithfulness or pledge of undivided love on the part of the accused partner does not appease his anger or suspicion. Whether the partner is really unfaithful or not is unimportant in determining if a person is suffering from insane jealousy. When anything and everything becomes proof of the sexual unfaithfulness of the partner, it is evident that a person is suffering with insane jealousy. The question of the faithfulness of the spouse becomes an obsession for a person gripped with insane jealousy. It may be said that an insanely jealous person **imagines** acts of unfaithfulness committed by one's spouse. He may suspect a familiar person as a potential rival or he may imagine a rival.

The term "partner" is interchangeable for spouse, lover, husband, wife, live-in friend or the like, engaged in a relationship which involves sexual intimacy. In this book the insanely jealous partner is referred to as "he"; and the accused partner as "she". In either case, the gender is reversible. Since, research indicates that there are two insanely jealous men for every one woman, the choice of the pronoun "he" over "she," in referring to an insanely jealous person, is warranted.

ACKNOWLEDGEMENT

Scores of people have contributed to the preparation of this book. Doris Lawson, and Jimmy Catlett, my friends and colleagues edited the first draft of the book, gave me encouragement, and contributed many valuable ideas. Dr. Sudhir Mendiratta most generously gave his time educating me in the use of the software utilized in the preparation of this manuscript and helped me in the overall format of the book. Jannie Mendiratta deprived her family of plenty of hours in the final editing of the manuscript.

I am indebted to Don Windham, Ph.D., Mike Meguiar, Ph.D, Rebecca Mobbs, Veena N. Gupta, Linda Rossmaier and others for exchange of ideas, observations, and for compilations of references at early stages.

Many people encouraged me to write this book and kept asking me when the book would be out. Their confidence in me worked as a constant source of energy and inspiration. For that, I am particularly indebted to Suzan Logsdon, Lana Whisman, Kathy Dills, Dave Franz, Linda Scott, Libby Thomas, Paul Hart, Debbie Whitmire, Yvonne Hubbard, Dianne Jackson, and many others.

I have taken tons of hours away from my family time and neglected the usual jobs and chores around the house. My family has admirably assisted me in providing concentrated attention to the jealousy project in the last two years (without feeling jealous!).

CONTENTS

In some cases, there are no secret lovers and there are no unfaithful spouses out there.

But jealous souls will not be answer'd so;

They are not ever jealous for the cause,

But jealous for they are jealous.

'Tis a monster

Begot upon itself, born on itself.

(Othello, III, IV, 160)

The jealousy of secret lover is inside the mind while the thorn of imagined infidelity sticks in the flesh, day and night.

Psychologists and Psychiatrists recognize it as a case of CONJUGAL PARANOIA or those who are more inclined towards literature call it OTHELLO COMPLEX. In common parlance, it is called INSANE JEALOUSY. Insane jealousy is irrational, excessive jealousy. It is the false entrapment of mind, an obsession with unfaithfulness of the person one loves; the hellish fire of doubt and distrust.

FOREWORD

Within limits, jealousy is a normal and acceptable emotion. In most societies, an individual who showed total lack of it would be regarded as odd, and a certain element of mutual jealousy is often seen as evidence of a healthy, involved relationship.

However, we all know that jealousy can become excessive. Sometimes this is perfectly understandable when, for example, a sexual partner is provocative, flirtatious with others, or downright unfaithful. Despite all the sexual freedom of the past three decades, possessiveness is still almost universally present in human relationships and so we are not surprised when someone reacts to this kind of situation with anger and jealousy. We can see this as normal human reaction, perhaps as an extension of our territorial sense, and in most cases the jealousy abates as the situation resolves itself.

At other times, the degree and duration of an individual's jealous feelings are so severe that they can only be regarded as evidence of illness. In the past, an abnormal degree of jealousy might have been construed as a specific disorder, but nowadays-- as Dr. Sharma clearly indicates-- it is known that it can be a symptom of a whole variety of psychological and emotional problems. When a clinician meets with a case, he or she knows that a careful assessment of the situation and of the person's mental state must be undertaken in order to understand the form the jealousy takes and whether or not it is symptomatic of a specific mental disorder. Then, hopefully, a worthwhile intervention can be undertaken.

Unfortunately, we do not always have the opportunity to intervene at the appropriate time, and the two harrowing stories told in this book show us just how pathological an individual's jealousy may become, and how we may be unable to avert its dreadful consequences. These kind of stories, unhappily, are not too uncommon. Even lesser degrees of abnormality may cause severe suffering, and we know that some victims of pathological jealousy can become housebound because they are terrified of another accusation of infidelity if they go out from the house; others may attempt suicide because they have reached the end of their tether. Many just keep their mouths shut and put up with the constant barrage of assault, sometimes physical as well as mental.

Abnormal jealousy is probably much commoner than we realize, but the victims do not complain in many cases out of embarrassment or fear, or-- in some cases-- ignorance of what is normal. Dr. Sharma does well to highlight the problem and to provide a detailed checklist of the symptoms and consequences of severe jealousy. Probably this will not change the jealous person's attitude even if he reads it, but it is important to educate the public, the concerned professional and, perhaps most vitally, the potential victim about what to look out for. In some cases, knowledge can truly avert tragedy.

The two case-histories make desperately sad reading, and they indicate the far-reaching effects of a jealousy which has reached such an extreme depth. It is my hope that Dr. Sharma's book will cast light on this relatively unknown area of human experience, that it will help professionals to recognize severe jealousy for the potentially dangerous emotion it is, and that it will encourage early intervention in situations where, otherwise, only human desolation can ensue.

Alistair Munro, M.D.

Dalhousie University,
Halifax,
Nova Scotia, Canada.

Professor Alistair Munro is an international psychiatric expert who has served on the Advisory Committee of the American Psychiatric Association.

PREFACE

Life has shortchanged many people via the medium of insane jealousy (a colloquial name for disorders of jealousy). A wife, loyal, and deeply in love, is rudely shocked by the accusations, hurled at her by her husband. Thereafter, she loses her freedom to talk, move, smile, or to act naturally and spontaneous around people. She is aware that she is under the constant surveillance of her spouse. She stands accused and faces the rage of a "wronged" spouse in spite of her absolute faithfulness and extreme cautiousness. Insane jealousy occurs in women as well as men. We will, however, use the masculine pronoun as it occurs more widely in men. An insanely jealous person threatens, cries, begs, and may even assault his spouse, all in his desperation to make her stop this imaginary betrayal. He breathes under the fear of adultery. He is unable to love because of his fear and rage. He lives under constant agony and torture of a self-created false belief. He is not cheated by his spouse. He is cheated by insane jealousy.

Relatives of the opposite sex are close suspects and may often be accused. All members of the extended family of the suspected spouse may be included in this elaborate suspicion of misconduct. Children of an insanely jealous family get short shrifted, too. They only get to relate to a part of their parents. The wholeness of family relationships is missing. One parent is all wrapped up in investigating, accusing and demanding confessions from the spouse of unfaithfulness. The other parent is busy defending against the onslaught of accusations. A mother is too scared of expressing love to her own children in the fear of making their father furiously jealous. An insanely jealous father may withhold love and affection from a child because he suspects that the child is fathered by some other man. Worse, he may carry an irrational grudge towards this child. Children of an insanely jealous father are afraid of expressing love towards their mother. They do not know when a seemingly trivial remark in conversation may set off a series of delusional fears in the mind of the insanely jealous and result in a full blown rage. "Being around my father was like walking on egg shells," says a child of an insanely jealous father. "We could not talk to mother alone." Another child from a similar family setting says, "When my parents are old and gone, all we would remember about them would be that my dad was cussing and my mom was crying."

Some women are driven to suicide or a suicidal attempt due to the unhappiness and hardship caused by insane jealousy of their spouse. Such a suicidal attempt, in the emergency room, or at the psychiatric clinic, may be identified as a result of "depression", or, a "marital problem". Similarly, some men are driven to suicide or a suicidal attempt due to the imagined indiscretions of their spouses. The problem may not be correctly identified in the preliminary evaluations.

The mission of this book is to explain that insane jealousy is a mental illness. It is to enable lay persons as well as professionals to recognize problems, characteristics, and behaviors of an insanely jealous person and his afflicted family. We want to assist individuals who are insanely jealous so that they may get in touch with the suffering of their own selves and accept help. We hope to enable families to break the barriers of shame and embarrassment. The success of this effort will be measured by how many members of afflicted families seek help in their own right and/or for the sake of their family members who are sick. By the same token, it is important that professionals acquire specific knowledge and skills, so they can help these families and individuals. For others, I hope, there is sufficient information in this work to recognize the consequences of insane jealousy and "nip it in the bud" before they get carried away with the passion of jealousy.

The life of a family with insane jealousy is shrouded in secret pain. It is our wish to share that pain and hope with our readers.

EXCESSIVELY JEALOUS PARTNER

DO THESE SOUND FAMILIAR TO YOU?

Here, in brief, are the signs of excessive jealousy. Do you recognize them? Presence of any **one** sign indicates presence of excessive jealousy. However, one sign alone does not determine the absence or presence of "insane jealousy" (disorders of jealousy). If a person exhibits **several** of the following behaviors, he or she may have a disorder of jealousy:

1. Extremely moody. Mood swings related to rage towards the partner.

2 At times extremely quiet and withdrawn from the partner.

3. Watches and monitors partner's actions and movements closely.

4. Does not allow the partner out of sight.

5. Spies on the partner.

6. Intolerant of friends and relatives. Especially intolerant of partner's friends and relatives.

7. Intolerant of compliments paid to the partner.

8. Intolerant of affection or attention expressed towards the partner by others.

9. Sudden and unexpected outbursts of rage related to jealousy.

10. Repeatedly doubts and accuses partner of unfaithfulness without reason or basis.

11. Questions with intense severity about the time spent in his or her absence.

12. Questions scathingly about partner's amorous relationships with people at work.

13. Relentless and untiring questioning of the nature of partner's premarital relationships, or of previous relationships, if unmarried.

14. Keeps close track of partner's time, travel, and pocket money.

15. Directly accuses partner of unfaithful behavior.

16. Insistently demands confession from the partner of sexual misconduct.

17.　　Enraged if the false beliefs about partner's unfaithfulness are challenged.

18.　　Abusive and assaultive towards the partner.

19.　　Disallows the partner from all outside contact and communication, such as from going out, picking up mail, receiving phone calls, etc.

20.　　Doubts the paternity of one's own children.

21.　　Suspects that partner is trying to harm or get rid of him or her to lead a lustful life.

22.　　Becomes anxious that the partner has or is going to develop a venereal disease due to her indiscreet behavior.

23.　　Suspects that the partner has lost sexual interest in him because of her interests elsewhere.

24.　　Believes that the partner is some sort of maniac with an insatiable hunger for sex.

THE VICTIM PARTNER

ARE YOU A VICTIM OF INSANE JEALOUSY?

Here are the signs that a victim of insane jealousy is likely to manifest. Do you recognize any of these signs? You are a victim of insane jealousy, if you find yourself doing any one of the following:

1. **The sight of telephone makes you nervous.** You do not like the telephone to ring. You are afraid the caller might be asking for you which will upset your partner. You do not want to answer the telephone yourself so that you can give your partner every opportunity to verify and satisfy.

2. **Your being late from work amounts to adultery.** When you get late from work by completing the urgent assignment given by your boss, you dread to reach home. You are afraid how you will ever convince your partner that you were not meeting your lover.

3. **When you come home, you have to explain a lot.** You feel compelled to give details of every minute you spent and every person you met when you were out of your partner's sight.

4. **You are always very careful.** You try to act very carefully in talking to outsiders. You try to avoid any possible grounds for suspicion. You try to make light of partner's distrust and suspicion of you or blame yourself. No matter what you do you still end up being accused of betraying your partner.

5. **You would rather not go out of the house.** You do not want to go out on your own. You don't want to get out of your house, with or without your partner, because no matter what you do and where you go, your spouse is going to accuse you of "playing the old trick" on him.

6. **Friends and relatives make you nervous.** You avoid meeting your friends, male or female, and relatives, even your own parents, siblings, uncles and aunts, merely, to avoid incensing your partner.

7. **You wished the world did not have members of opposite sex.** You feel your world would have been safer then. You

feel uneasy talking to members of the opposite sex, whether they are familiar or unknown to you. If you could, you would let your partner talk to them.

8. **You can't be natural and spontaneous with your own children.** You do not feel free to express your love to your own children lest you make your partner jealous. You are afraid of receiving love from your own children; you discourage its expression towards you and guide it towards your partner.

9. **The idea of being alone with someone terrifies you.** You are afraid of being alone with anyone, even with your closest relatives, lest you provoke jealous rage in your partner.

10. **You do not want to do make up or dress pretty.** You are afraid of getting in a pretty outfit, doing make up or looking attractive lest you upset your partner.

11. **Getting back in time is a matter of life and death for you.** If you must get out, you feel desperate to get back home. You fight against all odds so that you can make it in the time that is expected of you by your partner. The idea of being late ties knots in your stomach.

12. **You are still guilty.** No matter how careful and prudent you act, you still end up being suspected or accused of unfaithfulness by your partner.

THE EYE OF THE TIGER

After forty years of marriage a man shoots point blank into his wife's head and kills her. The penitentiary seems a foregone conclusion for the defendant. For the purpose of the court, justice needs to be meted out. After all, in the eyes of the law and the society, he is a killer. But how should the family look at it? Times such as this require us to choose sides, to feel sorry for one and angry with the other. We cast one in the role of villain and empathize with the helplessness and suffering of the other. But, the children of this family are the children of a victim and a killer at the same time. They are torn and bewildered. He was a caring father. He was a good provider for the family. Yet, a chilling tension always existed at home. But why, they would ask? How could he do such a thing to his own wife and their mother? While the family grappled with these questions, I was asked by the defense attorney to evaluate the defendant and advise the judge if this was a malicious, premeditated act, or a crime of passion. I saw the defendant. He came across to me as a responsible, conscientious, old man--a gentleman. I met the members of his family and carefully covered his early background. I gathered the details of the forty years of their marriage and came to the conclusion that this was a case of CONJUGAL PARANOIA.

Incredible as it may sound, this dastardly act was indeed caused by a delusional jealousy, a jealousy, that had reached the proportions of insanity. This gentleman had a specific mental disorder, identified in psychiatry as the delusional (paranoid) disorder of jealousy. In common parlance, this condition is referred to by some as "insane jealousy." I explained to the court that all of his delusions and the extraordinary jealousy, which, of course, had reached the degree of insanity, was directed towards one person alone, and no one else. That one person was his wife. There was only a rare chance that he would ever direct this much fury and jealousy, or love, for that matter, towards any other person. He, in my opinion, was no threat to society.

The judge had not encountered a similar situation before; nonetheless, he listened to the findings of this evaluation sympathetically. At the conclusion of the trial, the man was returned to society to live with one of his children. Having preyed on its victims, jealousy, the eye of the tiger, was closed, or so I thought.

Then occurred another incident a couple of years later, in a different town, with a different family. One morning, two women, unsuspectingly, came to check on their parents. They honked their horn but their parents did not come out. They entered the yard. As they walked to the porch, they found one body disemboweled and another body with its head blown off! The father first killed their mother and then turned the gun on himself. Shocked, stunned, dizzied, and then plagued with the nightmares and flashbacks, the two daughters came to me for help. As I began to work with them, I could not shake loose the thought of the loss of three lives, one life in the first episode and two lives in the second.

It kept haunting me. Three lives were lost and each time I was called to be involved. I said to myself, surely, I had missed something in the first episode. In the court, where I was testifying as an "expert" to explain the causes of the first tragedy, I went on to say that the condition of conjugal paranoia was extremely rare. Therefore, not many people know about it. I told them that the only other time I had professionally encountered this condition was twelve years ago, five thousand miles away, in the land of the British Isles. Now I stood corrected. I needed to revise my theories. It may not be as rare as I had previously thought.

In a matter of two years, it had struck twice in the realm of my professional experience. In the first of the two incidents, my role was confined to evaluate the mental status of the defendant and subsequently to do a periodic evaluation at the clinic to monitor the emergence of delusional symptoms, if any. During his visits to my clinic, I felt his loneliness and isolation; but he did not communicate any emotional side of this. I did not know if he was grieving, regretting, or missing his deceased wife. Whenever I broached this issue, he would change the subject or he would want to talk about his physical problems. But this time I was working closely with the victim's survivors. Their pain, their suffering and agony was incredible and inescapable. Yet they were fighting with bravery and composure, which won my admiration and at times moved me deeply. Here in the counseling session, I was only witnessing the suffering that befell them after the "murder-suicide" of their parents. But there was another suffering which they shared in the therapy sessions. This suffering had gone on life long - ever since they could remember.

The two daughters had been experiencing fear and pain which resulted from that gnawing, ever present suspicion of their father towards their mother. The father was absolutely convinced in his mind of his wife's infidelity and deception. All their lives, they had witnessed the indignity and humiliation that their mother suffered in the face of continuous accusations and charges of infidel acts supposedly committed behind his back. Any assurance from their mother would amount to lying. If the daughters tried to assure their father of their mother's upright conduct and her loyalty to him, it meant to the father that they were taking sides with their mother.

I came to realize that such fears and pain is not the only toll these unfortunate families pay. They also pay another heavy cost. They bear the loss of precious parental love that all children need for their emotional nourishment. One of the two daughters, who was the oldest child in the family, was disclaimed by the father as one of his own children. I still have not fully fathomed the depth of despair in a child whose father suspects that she is fathered by another man. One does not know if it makes it better or worse that "father" does not have a name and cannot be available to the child in flesh and blood. At any rate, my client, as a child, overheard profuse explanations on the part of her mother to convince the father of his paternity and she also heard her father's disclaimers in response. She grew up feeling as an unwanted child.

Through the two daughters, I was getting a closer look at the children from a family with insane jealousy. I was pondering over the fate of their parents. Was there something that I needed to do, when I was called by the attorneys in the aftermath of the first tragedy? At times, I heard a voice of self-reproach within, "Had I drawn the attention of the public and the professionals to the first one, this family would have sought some sort of help before it was too late." After all, the distance in location of these two families was not that wide. If both these families had sought professional help in time, could these deaths have really been prevented?

How do you persuade a family to go outside for its internal problem and seek professional help? How do you make an insanely jealous person see that he has a disorder, that it is all in the mind, that his wife is okay, and it is he who needs help? Hundreds of questions of this nature infested my mind. By the twist of fate or some strange happenstance, I felt I had been given the task to explain to the grieving families if their loved one was really a killer or just a very sick man. I felt I had the obligation to do something to facilitate this task, but I could not decide what that "something " should be.

In the meantime, the two daughters, Sabrina and Ashley, the co-authors of this book, went about their lives, putting up a brave front, taking care of their own families and of the unfinished business for the deceased. And then something totally unexpected happened. Several friends and acquaintances confided in them that a similar situation of relentless distrust and questioning of their faithfulness was occurring in their family! Many times, suffering becomes the basis of sharing. People can open their hearts to someone who has been there, has known it first hand, and still better, has paid the price. Sabrina, Ashley, and I are amazed and continue to be increasingly impressed with just how widespread the problem is. It is only through Sabrina and

Ashley that I first came to suspect the wide prevalence of insane jealousy. By now, each one of the contributors has been individually told of this "strange secret" by so many people that we are awed by the magnitude of the problem.

As I was writing this book, another woman came to me for crisis counseling. She had come two other times to the mental health clinic with her husband to seek help. Each time they were treated for "marital tension," "depression," and "alcohol and substance abuse." There was not even a mention of a jealousy disorder. This time, the third time, when she came to a mental health professional, she had already lost her husband. He committed suicide due to the intolerable jealousy, his rage, and depression. "Holly," the spouse of this very troubled man has contributed her story in "My Husband."

During the two years of researching, treating, and writing about pathological jealousy, I have come to be personally involved in the evaluation or treatment of many delusionally jealous patients or of the spouses who are affected by this problem. Public awareness of the problem is almost nonexistent. Experts, too, have little information or understanding of the problem. Their estimates of the prevalence of delusional jealousy appear to be far too short of the actual mark. According to the estimates by the psychiatric experts, there may be only about 69,000 to 115,000 people in America who are suffering from delusional disorders at any given time. Bear in mind that in these figures, the experts are including the entire classification of delusional (paranoid) disorders. The delusional disorder of jealousy is just one out of five types of delusional disorders. According to these estimates, the number of people suffering with the delusional disorder of jealousy type is expected to be even smaller. Experts do view it as a rare mental disorder. But, is it? In my opinion, experts have severely underestimated the prevalence of the delusional disorder of jealousy. Such an underestimation is due to a severe underreporting of the problem by the affected persons and failure in identification of the disorder on the part of the professionals.

However, a delusional disorder is not the only disorder of jealousy. Insane jealousy is found in many other emotional-mental disorders. Many depressed, anxious, and insecure patients are particularly prone to insane jealousy. Chronic and severe abuse of alcohol and other mood changing substances may also result in insane jealousy. Chronic physical illness, disability, impotence, brain dysfunction, extraordinary stress, mental or physical impairment, migration, deafness, blindness, conditions too numerous to mention, may cause or accompany insane jealousy. Countless women are beaten up by men in jealous rage. "Domestic strife" or "Domestic violence" is almost another name of possessiveness and jealousy. Just from what I have come to experience in a radius of fifty miles of my professional practice, I suspect there are hundreds and thousands of people, as couples and families in America today, whose lives are reduced to untold misery and unhappiness because of insane jealousy.

Many spouses are caged and imprisoned in their own homes because of this problem. There are wives who cannot go out to meet their friends or relatives on their own or even with their children. Members of the extended family may be secretively or openly shunned and detested. Everyone is suspected as being an accomplice or a confidante to the partner's sexual misconduct. Where insane jealousy strikes, husbands secretly monitor the mileage on the odometers to compare the actual distances of places that their wives said they visited. Telephones are bugged without the knowledge of their wives. The duration of absence from home is compared with the actual time taken to perform the tasks, to investigate the truthfulness of the spouse. The partner under suspicion has to remember every detail, the exact amount of time taken for each task, and the exact sequence of what they said or did in the absence of the insanely jealous spouse. Many are physically abused due to the rage resulting from the insane jealousy. All these tragic events take place when there is not even a shredof an objective evidence that a secret affair is taking place. Nor does there have to be a history of infidelity in the past.

In fact, when an insanely jealous person does not find any evidence, he is infuriated. He thinks that the "unfaithful" spouse is being really smart and deceitful, and has taken care of whatever evidence had existed. He demands confession from her. He desperately hopes that things will be straightened out if she just takes the right step, just goes ahead and confesses her misconduct. He sees his partner as a sex maniac who is interested in having sex with anyone and everyone around, except with him who rightfully must expect absolute attention and loyalty from her. The partner is expected to be ready and willing to satisfy all of his whims and desires at all times. If she does not do that, it confirms his suspicion that she, in fact, is not loyal and faithful to him. Many victims are working hard, day and night, to assuage these suspicions and to hide their embarrassment from outsiders. It is a secret with which the family contends, it has to live with. The members in the family try to cope by overlooking it for their sake and covering it up from everyone else.

Before everybody gets too anxious and starts wondering, "Am I insanely jealous?" or, "Is my spouse insanely jealous?" let us further clarify the condition of insane jealousy. People at one time or another will have passing doubts and suspicions regarding their lover or spouse. We all, now and then, entertain some feelings of jealousy when we see our partners taking more than an ordinary interest in another person, spending more than the usual time, or paying special attention to someone else. If somebody claimed that he or she never felt jealous, we would suspect the validity of such a claim. Insane jealousy is more than doubts and suspicions that people entertain one time or the other about their romantic partner. It is not to be mistaken with the lingering suspicions of unfaithfulness after an actual occurrence of infidelity. Those behaviors may be considered as behaviors of normal jealousy. Insane jealousy means that a person has an irrational belief regarding the unfaithfulness of a spouse or a person with whom one is romantically involved. This irrational belief is accompanied by an immense preoccupation and obsession with investigating and collecting evidence of the acts of unfaithfulness. When a person loses the objective reasoning to dismiss unfounded doubts and suspicions, when the issue of sexual unfaithfulness becomes an obsession, when a person seeks undue control of another person in fear of the commission of unfaithful acts, then, we can be certain that we are witnessing insane jealousy. Note that the emotion of jealousy is normal but insane jealousy is not. While we learn to accept and tolerate normal jealousy, we should definitely address the problem of insane jealousy. I want to be very careful in defining the problem and its consequences because I do not want to create any sensationalism about this problem. It is a fact that insane jealousy can kill. Perhaps, the outcome of this illness is far more serious and fatal than what we, as a society, have credited it with so far. Domestic violence is rampant in our society. More people are killed by friends and relatives than they are by strangers or unrelated people. We believe that insane jealousy is a major cause to reckon with in cases of intimacy-related murder and suicide.

In some cases, outsiders will not suspect anything is wrong with insanely jealous persons. They may appear very normal at work, business, and in all social relations. It is in the relationship with their spouses that insane jealousy is seen at work. In other forms of mental illness, a disturbance is seen in several areas of life-functioning and the abnormal behavior is too obvious to be missed by the family. If a severely mentally ill person makes similar fantastic charges, the accused wife can console herself that her husband is not in his right mind, therefore, she may try to ignore the abnormal behavior. But a woman whose husband seems normal in other respects, is often nagged by the question, "What am I doing that has caused this problem?" Some women observe stifling self-imposed restrictions upon their own selves due to fear or misguided guilt. Life for such women can become an imprisonment. Unfortunately, in families where a victim-spouse fears retaliation in form of violence towards herself or her children, or is unable to support the children, she does not perceive divorce as an option. So let us not ask her, "Why didn't you take the children and leave? Why didn't you divorce him?" Let us not charge her that she must have liked all the fuss that her husband made over her.

In my perception, the magnitude and shame of this problem is similar to that of child abuse. At one time, child abuse, too, was a family's foolproof secret. No one talked about it. It was not supposed to exist. But one day someone blew the whistle. From that moment, the floodgates started opening. Hundreds of thousands of cases have come to light since then. The problem of child abuse is being recognized and society is developing a machinery to handle it. Now, many families and children are getting help. The problem of child abuse is open for modification and in many cases can be prevented in the early stages. Now we can expect that some children will never come to be abused as a result of more open communication of the problem, community education, and professional and social intervention. Similarly, we are writing this book in the hope that the couples and families can share their grief and overcome their embarrassment. Our objective is to help people recognize insane jealousy and talk about it openly without the embarrassment and the belaboring of defense. Above all, we hope insanely jealous persons can get the help they need. They certainly are emotionally troubled as are the members of their families.

I hope that this book draws the attention of our society and the professional community in proportion to the seriousness of the problem. In this work, I intend to provide a start-up kit for further education, prevention, and treatment of insane jealousy.

I am now going to present two real life stories told by persons, who had a family member who was insanely jealous. Each one of them gives a first hand account of their experience with the insanely jealous family member and how it affected the family life. "Mother and Dad" is a story told by two daughters, Sabrina and Ashley, of their insanely jealous father. They had known for many years that Dad was abnormally jealous and suspected Mother without a due cause. From a professional perspective, their father had a mental disorder, a disorder of jealousy, or more specifically, a jealous type delusional disorder which we will define in the later part of the book. The story of Mother and Dad is the story of trials and tribulations of the two daughters of a jealousy afflicted family and their extraordinary experiences. In "My Husband," a wife, Holly, tells the story of how her husband, over the years of marital life, became more and more insanely jealous. The husband provides us an example of morbid jealousy, the insane jealousy without the delusion of infidelity. In his case, insane jealousy was there from the beginning of the relationship, but laid dormant for a while, then thrived with chronic depression and heavy substance abuse. Unfortunately, both the stories ended in the ultimate tragedy, death. They did not have the knowledge that the member of their family suffered from a disease and that this disease has a name, jealousy disorder. This disease can be treated and controlled. They are telling their stories to us so that others can benefit and they can find a meaning and purpose in their suffering.

All names and personal details are changed to protect the true identity of the characters.

MOTHER AND DAD

Insane jealousy of the father of Sabrina and Ashley became apparent to their mother soon after the marriage, if not before. He was accusing her of unfaithfulness and adultery with any man with whom she came in contact whether before their marriage or after. He continued disbelieving that Sabrina was fathered by him until she came to have an undeniable resemblance to him.   During the first few years of marriage, break up of marriage seemed imminent. One separation lasted for about three months. Father came back with promises to make it up to her and pled with her to give their marriage another chance. The two daughters did not notice any major problems for a while. Then, the accusations, periods of moodiness, and the jealous rage started again. From all accounts, father's mother was definitely a jealous person and most probably, insanely jealous. It is likely that the family of origin contributed to his disorder. Perhaps the Dad and his parents fostered and shared with one another false negative beliefs about Sabrina and Ashley's mother. After Dad's parents passed away, it seemed accusations and episodes of jealous rage subsided for a period and then reappeared. Mother for most part of the 47 years of marriage put up with the unpredictable nature of insane jealousy. She imposed many restrictions on herself. She never drove. She hardly ever went anywhere on her own and avoided contact with other men to forestall accusations of unfaithfulness. Their father's jealousy was delusional jealousy. He suffered from the Delusional (Paranoid) Disorder, Jealous type. Twenty-five years before he killed their mother and took his own life, he reluctantly went to a psychiatric hospital (the one and only admission to a psychiatric unit) on the insistence of his wife and relatives. At the hospital, their mother described him as someone who always had been a jealous person. He repeatedly told them that his wife was running around with other men and he would first kill her and then kill himself. Hospital staff noted his nervousness, depression, lack of sleep, and his preoccupation with the obsessional idea of his wife's infidelity. Not enough awareness existed at the time, about the delusional disorder of jealousy. His condition was diagnosed as that of psychotic depressive reaction. He was treated for psychotic depression with little success. He left the hospital without permission. He told them that he could not live with his wife's unfaithfulness any longer but that he could not leave her either. This, he said, did not leave him any choice but to kill her and kill himself. For twenty-five years, he tried to live with the impossible situation that was created by his delusion of unfaithfulness before he ended it all.

Names and other details have been changed to protect the true identity of the persons involved. Various parts of the first chapter of Mother and Dad, "Growing Up Under The Shadow Of Jealousy," are written individually by Ashley and Sabrina. Since this chapter relates to their early years, the experience of the growing years for each one of them was drastically different. The only way it could be represented accurately was for it to be written individually. To point out which growing experience belongs to whom, a heading is given as, Sabrina's Story, or Ashley's Story. The other two chapters, "The Last Few Days" and the "Aftermath And The Healing Of Wounds" are written jointly.

GROWING UP UNDER THE SHADOW OF JEALOUSY

In memory of our parents and with great love, we are putting our feelings down on paper, trying to heal scars from childhood until now. This is not meant to hurt anyone but hopefully help some see and identify a very serious problem. Over and over in our minds, we wonder why our family has suffered so much. We grab for answers, just some reason.

Sabrina and I find ourselves alone now at the age of forty-six and forty years. Last summer we experienced a tragic shock by finding our mother and dad dead, a murder-suicide. Dad had shot our mother twice with a 12- gauge shotgun. Then by propping the gun between his feet, he had killed himself. That sight has been hard to live with; it is always in our minds. The scene keeps flashing back and we relive that horrible day. Since then Sabrina and I, through counseling, have tried to cope, find answers and try and understand why it happened. Through counseling, we have been able to talk about our childhood and family life, trying to find a reason for Mother and Dad's death and why our brother at the age of forty took his own life?

Our aim is to try and help others to see the problem, so that they can be able to talk about it and do something to make things better. Don't be as secretive as we were. If we had been open about it, things might have been different.

Our dad was the second oldest in a family of seven children. Growing up during the Depression, Dad and his older sisters, at an early age, had to take on responsibilities. After Dad's two older sisters were married, at the age of twenty-four, Dad married our mother. She was twenty-one and the oldest child of five. She too knew what hard work was. Dad and Mother settled on the family farm in a little shack set off in the woods. As Dad's other sisters and brother married, they left the farm to find work and settled elsewhere. Since Dad and Mother were working the farm, our grandparents told Dad that if he and Mother stayed there, they would give Dad forty acres of the two hundred plus acre farm. Dad and Mother accepted this offer. They began cutting timber and planning to build a house.

Our father and mother were hard workers, working the fields together. As farmers, they had cattle, grew tobacco, acres of strawberries, corn and hay to feed the cattle, and always had a garden for the family's winter food supply. For a few hours each day, Mother had a job as a cook in the school which was right next to the farm. Then in the afternoon, the school was to be cleaned. The cleaning of the school was a family job. Dad had a side job driving a truck for a construction company, so he sometimes had long days.

We have gone over our childhood and our experiences in great details with each other. We have heard that even though two siblings grow in the same family, with the same parents, their life experiences are very different. It is certainly true in our case. Therefore, we decided to give our childhood reports separately.

SABRINA

I, Sabrina, can remember a lot of fussing and arguing and Daddy accusing Mother of having other men. He said that my brother before me, who died a few hours after his birth, was not his child. He said that I was not his child either. I used to hear this a lot. It made me feel unloved by both of them. I felt that if I were not around they wouldn't have problems. I didn't know what to do or say. I used to say, "Daddy don't be mad at Mother," and he would yell and push me away. I used to go and hide when they would start fussing. I'd go where I couldn't hear them. I would get under a bush or behind the food cellar and curl up in a ball like a scared dog and cry, sometimes crying myself to sleep. Then I would wake up with Mother and Dad yelling at me. I would come out and I would get a whipping for hiding. I tried to tell them why I hid, to get away from their yelling and fussing. But they would say they didn't want to hear it. They would say, "Don't you know you had us scared because we couldn't find you?"

Other times when the yelling started between Dad and Mother, I would get on the bed and sometimes under the bed. It was so bad that even with my fingers in my ears I could still hear it. I felt like a see-saw, not knowing if every day would be like that. But it was good for a week or so and then it would start again. Every time they got into a fuss, it was the same thing over and over, my older brother and I were not his and he always brought up the subject of "other men." Daddy would say, "What man has been here?" I felt unloved most of the time. When times were good, I got some love and attention. But when things weren't good, I got pushed away. Daddy's mad spells would last sometimes weeks at a time. Daddy would not speak to Mother. I would ask Mother, "What's wrong with Dad?" Mother would say, "He's not feeling good." So I learned not to ask as the years went on.

Daddy worked hard all of his life, making a living for his parents and for our family. Daddy always put his parents first. It seems like he never had time for us. On holidays,

Dad's sisters and brothers would have a good time while we would be in the fields hoeing tobacco or corn.

I can't remember much playtime in our childhood. I remember getting a doll when I was four years old, my first doll. I remember so well, it was a baldheaded baby with a diaper and top, and a blanket around it. I don't know what happened to that doll, it disappeared. I remember waking up crying, wanting my baby doll. I never did find her. I had something I could love and it was gone. I thought if my doll disappeared, so could my brother, Brian. So after that I watched Brian because he might disappear like my doll. I thought I couldn't let him out of my sight. When people would come around, we would hide behind the couch or chair and peak around.

My grandma used to say a lot, "These are my kids," just like Mother didn't exist. We had been through a lot. I used to dream about how I wished our family to be, with a lot of love, that our parents could get along, that they had good things to say to each other. We used to stay with our grandparents when we were young, while Mother and Dad were out in the fields.

I never saw Daddy push my younger brother Brian aside; he always had time to hold him and love him. I felt left out. It seemed like Daddy's world was around Brian, and when Ashley was born, Mother's around Ashley. I felt like an outsider looking in. I thought I was to blame for everything that was not right in the family. It got to the point that I believed I wasn't Daddy's child or I would have been treated better. I always wondered whose child I was. It broke my heart that I always seemed to be alone. I would always ask myself," Why doesn't someone love me? What can I do to make someone love me?" I was so hungry for love. I did extra things to help Mother in the kitchen. I thought that if I helped Mother a lot, it would be different.

My Dad let his parents and siblings run all over him all his life. In return, Daddy would blame Mother for things that didn't go right. Daddy's family was always running our mother down. Mama and Papa, our paternal grandparents, would even tell us that our mother was "not fit to be a mother. She is trash, her family is trash." Dad was running my mother's dad down. Daddy didn't have anything good to say about our mother's family. Mother wasn't allowed to have any of her family stop by to see us. Mama and Papa would report everything to Dad. Mother's family didn't come around very much because Daddy didn't make them feel welcome. Sometimes Dad had long days on his job. Mother would always have us kids something to eat after school so we could have supper together with Dad. The food would be kept ready and warm. But day after day, he would come in from work, not to us, but to his parents. The thought of not being most important to our Dad hurt us. By the time Dad came home to us, many times he would have already eaten, leaving us to have our supper without him.

There was lot of fussing going on. Mother was getting tired of eating alone and not having our own family time. Dad was making accusations based on what he was told by Mama and Papa about our mother. They reported to Dad all that went on, who, if anyone, including Mother's family was there during the day. Dad did not want anyone around. We can remember Dad telling Mother, "They (Mama and Papa) tried to get me not to marry you. They told me you were not good enough." All this time Mama and Papa were building within Dad delusional mistrust and resentment. Mother and we children had to compete with Mama and Papa for our Daddy's time, love, and attention. Also, we did chores for Mama and Papa, carrying in the coal for their heat stove, and water to the kitchen until it was finally piped into their house. We did what they told us to do. If we didn't, it was reported to Daddy.

I played basketball in grammar school. In high school, gym was my favorite class. I could get rid of my anger and frustration. Kids at school never would have thought I had any anger in me, because I was a quiet and shy person. I kept things to myself. I didn't talk about our family problems. I used to cry a lot. That helped to get rid of some of the hurt that I was feeling.

I prayed so much for things to get better. They did for a while. There were smooth times in between eruptions. It was like sitting on a time bomb, not knowing when it would go off next.

Once, when I was sixteen years old, after one of these eruptions, I said I was getting tired of this. I told Mother and Dad that they were hurting us kids, putting us through this over and over. I went in the bedroom and got the .22-rifle and ran out of the house, across the road, up over the hill, to the strawberry patch. Once there, I sat in the shed and cried with the gun sitting beside me. Mother came up not long after. She was out of breath. She said, "What do you mean by this?"

I said, "I don't know." I told Mother," I'm tired of all this fussing and accusing all the time. I am hurting because I don't know what to do to make things better." Mother said, "Do you think this will make it better? I said, "I really don't know."

Mother checked the gun. There weren't any shells in it. We talked for a while. I told Mother it would have been better if I had not been born. Mother told me to not talk like that. She said, "I love you kids. I guess I have not shown it especially to you. Yes, I know it probably hurts you more. You have been through more than Brian or Ashley."

We walked down the hill together. I was still sobbing. Lots of times I wanted to run away, but where could I go? "If my own family didn't love me how could someone else?" I thought. I grew up in my own family and yet I was alone.

When I was a junior in high school, my dad thought that someone was out to hurt me and rape me. He told this to me. To hear something like that, one can understand what that did to me. I was a shy person anyway. I was then scared to even walk to my aunt's house. Anybody who knew me knew that I didn't get to do much. There wasn't much I desired to do anyway. Even if I had wanted, I wouldn't have been allowed to go anywhere. The only way I got to go anywhere was to go with my aunt and my two cousins. The first time, I went to a drive-in movie was at the age of seventeen or eighteen and then I went with my aunt and cousins. I didn't go on a date until I was eighteen years old, and then my brother went with me. I didn't mind that since I wanted to just get out of the house now and then. There was this boy who hitchhiked to come to see me and to go to church with us. My brother was driving by this time, so we all drove to church together. That was our main activity together. Then I met another boy through my aunt. He started coming over on Sundays to see me. We would sit down in the family room, talk and watch some TV or go outside and play some basketball. Sometimes when he came over, we rode down to my cousin's for a little while. He would always have to go home before sundown. I met him when I was sixteen but didn't get to go anywhere with him till I was eighteen.

There was this one thing that stayed with us that happened when we were in our teen years. Mother and Brian took care of the barn work, feeding and milking. We drank unpateurized cow's milk. Mother, on her way from the barn, would stop to leave Mama and Papa milk from her bucket.

The day seemed ordinary; Dad came home from work, parked the truck in the driveway, got out and walked across the road to Mama and Papa's house, as usual. When he came home, he was very mad and accused Mother of putting "something" in their milk. It seems that Mama and Papa were accusing Mother of putting some kind of poison in their milk. Dad was believing it. They sent the milk off to be tested. All of Daddy's brothers and sisters, except one sister, Veronica, and her husband, Bob, supported this crazy accusation. These accusations and threats of seeing lawyers, trying to prove that Mother tried to poison them, went on for a year. We could not feel any love for them. All we were shown from them was hate and repulsion for Mother. Our grandparents kept Daddy torn up about this milk business and everything else that they could dream up. We remember Daddy coming home and telling our mother that Mama and Papa wanted her to leave. Our mother said, " I am not leaving. I did not do anything wrong and I did not poison that milk." One day my grandpa came over and yelled for us to come out. We could

hear our grandma in the background, telling him what to say.
He said they had enough proof against our mother to send her
to prison. He said he knew for sure that she had tried to kill
them. We wondered in our minds how Dad could just sit
there and let Mama and Papa hurt us. Grandpa yelled, "I
want your mother to leave. If she doesn't, then I want your
dad to get rid of her one way or the other."

We yelled back, "If you don't want our mother around,
then you don't want us. We won't be around either."

Grandma yelled from her front porch,"Leave and don't
come back." We do believe that if Mother had walked away
and left us, then they could have had Daddy all to themselves
to dictate and order around. Dad stayed with Mama and Papa
for a while, leaving us by ourselves. Finally, they gave him
an ultimatum, either get rid of our mother or leave. That's
when Dad decided that we would go to Arizona. We packed
all that we could on a U-haul. We left on the first of January,
leaving behind everything that Mother and Dad had worked
for together. In Arizona, Daddy found odd jobs and Mother
did babysitting. I, too, found a job to help with the expenses.
Mother and Dad made enough to buy groceries and other
things and I paid the rent. I thought, "Now I am doing
something to help. Maybe they will love me for helping
them. I should always try something or do something so they
can approve of me."

I met my husband, maybe, a week after our move to
Arizona. He took me around and showed me the city that we
had come to live in. Some evenings we went out but most of
the time, we were there at the house, watching TV. Just a few
days after our first date, he asked me to marry him. At this
point, trouble started again between Mother and Dad.
Mother had started babysitting to help buy groceries. She was
babysitting just in the apartments in the neighborhood. Dad
was doing odd jobs around apartments as a handyman. He
would be checking on Mother every now and then. Perhaps,
some problem developed around babysitting, we don't know.
We do know that as the weeks went on, accusations about
milk poisoning would come up, especially after Dad's brother

and his wife visited. Mother would cry a lot and would want to talk to someone from her family. Just to have someone talk to her, she would call collect her sister in Georgia. She had to be very careful, not to be caught by Dad. Many times, she would have to hang the phone up, not being able to finish the conversation or say good-bye.

Going to Arizona did not make any difference. The problem still haunted us. Just a couple of months after our arrival in Arizona, Mother decided to separate from Dad and go back to Georgia. Now, we had a most difficult decision to make: Which parent would we go with? Ashley loved Dad, Brian, and me on one hand and she wanted to stay in Arizona with us; but she loved her mother too and wanted to be with her if Mother was going. Similarly, I was torn between whether to go back with them or stay in Arizona. Unfortunately, it was time to choose sides. Andrew had already asked me to marry him. So, Dad, Brian, and I stayed in Arizona and Mother and Ashley went back to Georgia. Here, my would-be husband was asking me to hurry and make up my mind about marriage; he had come up with a specific date for marriage. So, I got married in just three months of our arrival in Arizona. While I was starting a new life, Daddy had still not got any steady work and Brian was not happy at school, so in about two months after my mother's leaving, Daddy and Brian also left for Georgia.

ASHLEY

Here in Georgia, I was surprised when Dad and Brian showed up one day. Dad and Mother again got back together. But we would not go back to the family farm. This was a condition of their getting together. Daddy got a job on road construction. Mother got a job cleaning houses for three to four hours a day. Many days, when Mother would get home, Dad would be next door, visiting our female neighbor. These visits were explained as just having a cup of coffee. Mother began to question these frequent visits, which would cause a fuss. Dad did not understand why anyone would be the least bit upset by his visits. However, his attitude, when it came to Mother, was in sharp contrast to what he applied in his own case. For example, one day Dad went to pick up Mother from one of her jobs. A brother of the lady of the house was there at the time, so Dad accused Mother of being in bed with him. These accusations became so severe and real in his mind that Mother had to quit working outside the house.

When Sabrina's first child was to be born, Mother went to Arizona to help. Later, after the birth of Sabrina's son, Dad went up to Arizona with a male acquaintance of his. After a few days, Mother and Dad returned to Georgia with this man. As soon as they reached home, Dad accused Mother of having an affair with this man, and Daddy was there at all times. Not long after that, Dad accused Mother of having an affair with another man. He called Sabrina on the phone in Arizona, telling her all about this. Mother wrote to Sabrina and told her that it was not true. When Dad called again, Sabrina told him that she did not believe Mother would do anything like that. Such is the nature of insane jealousy that Sabrina was still hearing it, even being that far away. From that time on, going home from school was horrible for me. The fusses and fights were constant. Dad would make a point of calling Mother a whore.

One day Mother and Brian came to check me out of school. Dad's sister who worked in a psychiatric hospital had come and had talked Dad into going to the hospital where she was employed. We were told that Dad was going to the hospital because of his "nerves." We also knew that his nerves were bad because of jealousy, and what he had imagined happening between Mother and a man in Paris, Georgia. Dad was depressed and upset, and somehow, his sister talked him into going to the hospital. There, Dad stayed for several weeks before he was given weekend passes to come home. Finally, there was peace at home.

Looking back, we now know that our Dad had insane jealousy. Even twenty-four years ago he had threatened to take his own life and Mother's life. We are sure that the doctors must have known about it. We can't understand why they didn't tell our mother about it; why they didn't do something more. They gave Dad some shock treatments, but that only made Dad's nerves and jealous accusations worse. We know that when Dad was in the hospital, he had a cut on his right wrist. Dad was left handed; it is obvious that he tried to cut his wrist with his left hand. He was convinced in his mind that our mother was unfaithful. He told the nurses and the doctors at the hospital that he could not live with our mother but he could not leave her either. In his mind there was no other solution. He told them that he would one day kill both himself and our mother. We wish the doctors had told us that Dad had threatened our mother's life.

Let us return to life at home. After his return from the hospital, Dad had not found steady work. He needed work and money to support the family. He had a cousin who had a dairy farm and an empty house for helpers. He asked Dad if he would like to work with him. So we made another move. Mother and Dad's day then started around four in the morning, when they had to milk some sixty cows. During the day, there was always work to do either sowing seeds or putting up feed for the cows. For me, this was the last year of high school, but I didn't care if I finished it or not. Dad had again brought up old accusations, and a few times had hit Mother in my presence.

Dad was again acting really wild. After he and Mother retired for the night, I could hear through the thin walls, Mother begging Dad to please quit, that he was hurting her. I was afraid to go inside their room. I wanted to get out of the house. After my high school graduation, I began to stay with my brother, Brian, and his wife to keep their son. The man I was dating and falling in love with was usually around when I was at my parents' home. Dad began to make remarks to me that my boyfriend, Chad, was after my Mother, not me. For no reason at all, and no matter who happened to be around, Dad was jealous of them. Anybody who talked to Mother or acted even the least bit friendly would make Dad intensely jealous.

My sister, Sabrina, recalls this about her school days, "I had friends who would talk to me about their problems, but I didn't talk about it to anyone. I couldn't talk about my problems at home either. My problems were worse than any that my friends had, so I kept them to myself. I used to wish that I could only have their kind of problems."

One night Dad told me that I was a whore, just like my mother was. I told Dad then that I had never seen any justifiable reason for him to accuse Mother of such things. I told him that I was proud of my mother. He said, " I don't know how you could be proud of someone like that." While I was away during the weekdays, there were times that Mother, out of fear, would go and stay the night with our cousins.

SABRINA

In Arizona, I was receiving letters and phone calls from Daddy begging me and my husband to move to Georgia. As he kept on, I gave in and we moved back to Georgia. At the time, my two sons were six and four years of age and my daughter was only four months old. We lived with Mother and Dad for a few months. While we were there, things seemed to be okay between Mother and Dad. However, we wanted to have our own place to live, so we bought a small place close to my parents. We would visit my parents once or twice a week. Sometimes, Mother would ask for my children to stay with them. Once, when my daughter was still a baby, Mother had brought her to spend the night with them. That night Daddy threatened himself and Mother. Mother told me that Dad had threatened her with a gun. I told Mother that I couldn't have my kids over there to spend the night again. I didn't want my kids to hear the fussing, like I had been exposed to as a child. I asked Mother what got Dad started again. She said that her sister had come to see her earlier. Dad did not like anyone from her family. So, when Mother's sister was visiting, Dad ran her sister down, and said that she was nothing but a troublemaker. As Mother and

I were talking, Dad came in and must have overheard some of this.

Dad said, "You are plotting against me." He told me that I was like my aunt and I believed everything my mother said. He asked me, "How can you believe anything your mother says, knowing what kind of person she is?" Daddy said that we were ganging up on him. Dad said that if I believed my mother, I should get out of the house and never come back.

So my husband, kids, and I left immediately. I was upset and crying that my own dad asked me to leave and never come back. I felt that moving here from Arizona was the worst mistake we had made. If it had not been for Daddy begging me to come back here to live, we probably would not have come back. Daddy would say, "Jobs are better back here." My husband agreed to move back here. He left a good job there. Here, both of us together were making less than what he alone was making in Arizona. Days later, Mother and Dad came over. Dad told me he was sorry for what he had said. He invited me to come back. But, it never could be the same for me after that. I was afraid to say much around Daddy as I didn't want to get run off again.

SABRINA AND ASHLEY

Going back to the grandparents' saga, just about this time, their family farm needed to be sold so the division of the property would be easier among their children. Our grandparents were getting old. Dad's brothers and sisters had no use for the land. Dad was the only one who was in the farming business. Dad went to them and talked up a deal. He offered to buy the land for the price they would get outside. Mama and Papa agreed. Dad went to a bank to get the loan. Everything was ready except signing the papers. The planned trip to the lawyer's office came to a sudden stop on the day that was scheduled for the final signing of the papers. Mama said that Dad's brother in Arizona would never be back in Georgia if they let Dad buy the farm. Dad, being a kind and loving person to his parents, said that if that was the way his brother felt about it, then he did not want the farm. Then he tried to buy the forty acres which were pledged to him earlier and were rightfully his. These were the forty acres that were pledged to him and Mother for taking care of the farm for all those years. But they refused to give him the land that he had earned as wages. Instead, it was sold to Dad's sister in Arizona. This was a turning point for Dad toward Mother. She was by his side. He could not believe his own family would do him so dirty. Finally he was feeling and seeing what his children and wife had suffered in the hands of his family. But Dad really loved his home place. He still loved Mama and Papa. When an adjoining farm was for sale, he bought it to live next to Mama and Papa. But Mama and Papa had a harder time trying to watch every move of ours from this house.

As Mama and Papa's health began to fail, they needed Mother's help. When Mama died, each child was taking turns staying a week with Papa. This began to be too much for some and they would ask Dad to take their week. When it got to be very frequent, Papa came to live with Mom and Dad. It was difficult to believe that our aunts and uncles would want our mother to keep and wait on their Dad, after they had said she tried to poison Mama and Papa. We were already married and living at our homes, and, at first, we found it very difficult to accept Papa in our parents' house. We could not love him since he and Mama had hurt us so much. But we began to feel sorry for him. He couldn't understand why his children didn't come more often. He was nearing eighty- two years of age. One day he told our mother he didn't know what he would have done without her. A tumor was growing around Papa's windpipe and as breathing was a problem, he had to be put in a nursing home for treatment.

Dad and mother went to visit Papa in the nursing home three to four times a week. Each time, when Dad and Mother went to visit him, Papa would beg to go home. That tore at my dad. As I sat with Papa one day, he became sad talking about his kids and made the remark, "If I had only known what I know now, things would have been different." That day, he spoke of his appreciation and love of both of my parents for keeping him. We wished he had realized that earlier. Not too many nights later, we sat there as Papa died. We wished that we could have loved and grieved our grandparents deaths, like grandchildren should, but we couldn't. We never felt loved by them.

Later, our aunt and uncle decided to sell the farm, but they would not sell it to Dad. An uncle in Arizona bought it. Before the sale Dad had used a pasture field on this farm, and fenced it at his own expense. After our uncle bought the farm, he leased it out to someone else. Dad and Brian tried to work something out so that Dad could still use the pasture, but it was no use. Our uncle was looking out for himself. Once, Uncle made the remark, "This is a dog eat dog world." Dad said,"But I am your brother."

While, Dad was being walked all over by others, we grew closer to each other. Dad and Mother were supporting each other and Brian was working with Dad. Brian never questioned Dad or disagreed with him on anything. He quietly listened to Dad, whatever Dad had to say. There were times when Dad would have one of his moody spells (rages of jealousy). But if there was a big fight between Mother and Dad, we didn't know it. The farm that Mother and Dad bought was looking better as they worked hard tending it. They cleaned and cut brush and took care of every little detail. They took so much pride in it, not minding the work. Time and time again, we would see Daddy looking out the window toward the home place. We don't know how he kept from feeling resentment toward them. We witnessed so much unfairness that it was no wonder Dad and Mother were always reminding us, "Do unto others as you would have them do unto you, not as they do to you."

Then a very unfortunate thing happened in the life of our family. Our brother, Brian, committed suicide in the prime of his life. It was totally unexpected. We all were shocked. Dad grieved a lot over Brian's death. He put Brian's picture on the table, next to his chair. It was his wish to have Brian's picture at a place where he could see it all the time. He dwelt on his death. This grief ate at Dad and he was never able to accept it. However, he did not see that mother was grieving too. Once, Dad made the statement to Mother that Brian's death didn't seem to bother her. Mother said she tried to be strong for Dad, so she did not cry in front of him. Mother cried and grieved when she was around us. Brian's death brought so much change in our lives. Dad's and Mother's spirits were broken. Mother tried to be the unfailing support for Dad. Their love seemed to grow stronger. An incident took place which, we think, helped Daddy to believe in our mother. In 1987, Dad was mowing the yard which has a slanting bank. The riding mower began to roll backward, then turned over, landing on Dad. Miraculously, the blade was turned up, so he was able to shut the motor off. The blade gear had punctured his leg. He had numerous bruises and scrapes. Mother was able to lift the riding mower and free Dad from under it. She called neighbors and then an ambulance to transport Dad to the hospital. We went to meet them at the hospital. That day, we saw more love between them than ever before. Things seemed good all around.

Jealousy was not as great a problem in the last couple of years as it was in the previous years. We could relax and say that our family was happy like anyone else's family. It is true that the problem of jealousy was not completely gone. In the last couple of years, Dad would start accusing mother and questioning her, but that would always stop after a week or two. Unfortunately, in the last few months, it got really bad.

One day, just out of nowhere, these questions started coming out of Dad, "Who was that who was coming to the house?" when he heard someone passing on the road, or "Who is that man who was turning and leaving?" "Why did he want to see you?" if someone on the street was coming and turned around near our driveway. Once the accusations and the questioning started, they never stopped. In the past, such questioning and accusations would stop after a week or so.

Throughout their lifetimes, we were really close to our parents. We saw them at least once a week and generally, more than once a week. We were a close-knit family. However, being born in a family where a parent is so jealous, it brings additional responsibilities on children. We had to be very careful that we did not arouse Daddy's suspicion or make him jealous. We learned how to be very careful and not say anything that could go wrong if he was in one of his "moods". Sometimes, any little thing could set him off. We were always careful about the following things:

Not to spend more for Mother's birthday, Mother's Day, or Christmas gift than we did on Daddy's. Most of the time, we ended up spending more on Daddy for gifts of this nature.

To show more affection to Mother than we did to Daddy. For example, Daddy might think that we were hugging Mother tighter and longer than we did him. It was okay if a hug or a kiss was less for Mother, but it could not be more.

To watch our facial expressions. Daddy was suspicious that some secret might be going on or we might be trying to keep things from him.

To spend the same amount of time with each of the parents, and as much as was possible, with both of them in the same room.

To be present until Dad returned, if we visited Mother in his absence. Sometimes, we would go to visit Mother during the day, while Dad was at work. Mother would always want us to stay until Dad came home, so he would know that it was we who had been there and not someone else.

Not to laugh or to be funny, unless Dad was in the mood for such things. So, we had to see and test him out first. Most of the time, we waited for him to make the first move for conversation. As we came in, we asked him how he felt. By that we knew how to interpret his mood, and if we could say much that day or not.

If anybody was being friendly or funny, Dad wanted to know what was going on, what they were talking about, or what it was that was so funny. He was suspicious of everyone: Mother's sister, friends, neighbors, and even us kids. Many times, Dad would sleep in the chair when we were visiting. We really think that he merely pretended to sleep, so he could hear what we would say about him.

Mother, of course, had to watch her every move. We observed that even around us, her own children, she was very careful as to what she said and did. She was afraid to enjoy herself and laugh. She had to be careful how she sat or stood. Her clothes could not be tight. Clothes had to be thick enough so that undergarments could not be seen. When she wore a dress, she was always pulling it to make sure that her knees were covered.

Daddy put lots of restrictions on our mother. She was not allowed to do many things which women ordinarily do and take for granted. This was Daddy's way of controlling Mother. Some of the restrictions, Daddy put on Mother were:

When Daddy would go out, he would make a list of things for Mother to do. If she did not get them done, he wanted to know who had been there that she did not get enough time to do those things.

He told her what she could wear and what she could not. She could not shave her legs. She couldn't wear lipstick with bright colors. Only clear, or natural color lipstick was allowed. No other make-up was permitted. Similarly, she was not allowed to wear fashionable things, like glasses, fancy shoes or fancy clothes. She was not allowed to spend money on herself.

He did not want Mother to go anywhere without him. Lots of times he would restrict Mother from seeing her family with him or without him.

THE LAST FEW DAYS

Last Mother's Day was a happy one. That day, besides being Mother's Day, was also the annual day of our ancestral cemetery in which our brother, Dad's ancestors, many cousins, and friends were buried. This is an occasion when we decorate the cemetery, visit the graves, and spend some time in the memory of our loved ones. Therefore, every year on this particular day, Dad's brothers, sisters, their families, and close friends got together. On this Mother's Day, as on previous Mother's Days, practically everybody came. The day, as luck would have it, turned out to be beautiful and warm. We visited the cemetery in the morning. Thereafter, all our relatives and friends got together at Dad and Mother's place for lunch. We set up the picnic tables on the lawn under the large shade trees. We reminisced about old times and laughed together.

When evening approached, people started preparing to say their good-byes. As each one would get up to leave, we all would embrace one another and say good-bye till the next time. For some who lived long distances, it might be one whole year before we would get to see them again. We cleaned off the tables and the kitchen, so Mother would not have to do it later all by herself. Our husbands, Sabrina, and I were the last ones to leave. By then, we all were worn out and ready for a nap or just to hide somewhere for a little rest. Not in our worst fears could we have imagined that it was the last big family get together our parents were to host!

The following week was normal. That week on Wednesday night, as always, I visited my Mother and Dad for a while after the church service. But there was another reason to go there that evening; Mother and Dad had not come to the church. I kept on wondering that if they had not planned to come that evening, then why did they not let me know about it earlier. When I went there, I recall that Dad was very quiet and kind of distant; but I did not think much of it at the time. On the following Friday night, Mother, Dad and our families had planned to meet at a restaurant for the evening meal. Mother and Dad came to my house and they rode to town with me and my husband where we had planned to meet others. I noticed Dad was not himself. He was quiet and somewhat withdrawn. However, Dad got through the evening without anyone else seeming to notice or think anything of his mood. At any rate, everyone in the family knew that Daddy went into those "moods" especially when he felt bad. We were used to overlooking him when he had one of those moods. As soon as we brought Mother and Dad in our car to our home where their truck was parked, they hugged and kissed me and left for their home.

The following Sunday, we went to the church service. Mother, Dad, my husband, and I went to this church every Sunday. Close to the church is a cemetery where our Mother's parents and her ancestors are buried. This being the decoration day for this cemetery, as other years in the past, we were to skip the church school after the service and go to the cemetery where we would visit Mother's family. In the previous years, Dad, too, used to join us for the visit to the cemetery. As we were getting ready to leave the church, I asked Dad if he was going with us. Dad told me that he did not want to go. Mother, my husband and I went together to the cemetery. On the way, I found Mother to be quieter than usual. However, when we went there, Mother picked up and enjoyed talking to her sisters and friends. We stayed there for about an hour. As we started walking towards the car, Mother said, "Daddy is having one of his spells. We didn't go to bed at all last night. He told me not to tell you anything, but it's bad." At this point I didn't want to know and didn't ask any questions. We drove home in complete silence. My heart was dreading to think what the afternoon would be like for Mother on her return. I had already planned to stay with Mother and Dad for the afternoon before I came to know any of this. So I thought I should go ahead and stick to my plan. My husband went back to our home and I went to Mother and Dad's house.

As I walked in, I saw Dad sitting glumly at the dining table working on a puzzle. I tried to start a conversation with Dad, but he would only answer as briefly as possible. After a period of silence, Dad said, "Don't you want to know what's wrong with me, my being so quiet?"

I told him that I thought, maybe, I had said something to upset him, although I didn't know what that could be. Incidentally, it is true that lots of times, when Dad would look upset and quiet, Sabrina and I would wonder if we had said or done something which had upset him, or if his mood had to do with that same old stuff of baseless accusations about Mother. He then went on to ask me if Mother had not already told me what had happened. I knew that if I ever told him Mother had mentioned anything about it to me, he would be very suspicious and angry with Mother. Therefore, I plainly told him, "No, Mother did not tell me anything," and I asked him in return, "Why, what is going on?"

Upon which, he proceeded to tell me what a "whore" my mother was and always had been. He said that she could never be satisfied with just him and "all she thought about was sex! sex! sex!" Dad had worked it all out in his mind as to what exactly happened and how it happened. He had a specific time and a place, and a specific male with whom the act was committed. He had also conjured up some other fantastic visions of actual occurrence of adultery. His details were improbable. I knew that all he had to go by in thinking up these ideas was the fact that he was away from the house for a couple of hours. Nonetheless, it was futile to argue with Dad. Whatever he believed was right and what everybody else had to say about it was wrong. He believed in what he imagined about Mother and if you tried to tell him differently, he would become furious and think that you were taking Mother's side. Absolutely convinced that what he was saying was a fact, he told me, "If she would only admit to doing it, we can work it out." Mother came into the dining room at that time, and said, "Roy! you said we weren't going to upset the kids and now you are trying to turn them against me. I didn't do anything and I am not admitting to something I didn't do."

All this time, I was sitting there with my head in my hands, crying, not believing what I had heard and not able to say anything. My heart ached. The accusations we had heard all our lives and which seemed to have died down in the last couple of years were now coming back. In the last couple of years, I had thanked God so many times for the happiness that our parents finally had. We were content to see that their love had grown, and that they were closer than we could ever remember. But that afternoon, I felt that everything they had built together in these years was slipping away.

Although in the past, it had never worked and it seemed more difficult than ever to change Dad's beliefs in this matter, I still tried to reason with Dad. I tried to tell him that what he was saying could not in any way be true. But Dad could not be reasoned with. I kissed them and told both of them that I loved them. Not knowing what else to do or say, I left reluctantly. In the past, when Dad had made similar accusations and seemed upset, it took a week or so for things to become normal again. I consoled myself believing that things would be okay in just a few days.

When I came home, my husband and I discussed the problem that was going on between my parents. My husband and I agreed that Sabrina should also be told what was going on. Although Dad had told me that afternoon that he did not want Sabrina to know anything about it, we had to go against Daddy's wishes. Incidentally, we would never know the real reason why Dad did not want Sabrina to know about it. However, we have often wondered whether Dad was trying to protect Sabrina because she had just recovered from a severe illness. At any rate, my problem was that I did not see how I could handle it alone. I went ahead and told Sabrina. We decided to go up to Dad and Mother's, the next morning.

Come Monday morning, Sabrina came to my home and we started promptly to go to Mother and Dad, but we were not quite sure what we would say to them when we got there. We felt fear overtaking us. So we stopped at the country church where we always went as children. Sabrina and I knelt in front of the altar and prayed that God would give us the right words to say. At any rate, we were still feeling fearful about what we would encounter when we reached there. However, we were resolved that it was time to stand up and to take action. We nervously went to our car and drove up to Mother and Dad's.

When we pulled up into their driveway, we did not see the truck. We thought that Dad might have gone to run some errands but at least Mother would be there. The next thing we noticed was that both the doors were locked. We went up to the place where they hid an extra key. But there was no key!

We began to wonder where they could have gone. As we walked around and went up to the garden, we came to a spot where a large amount of papers had been burnt. In the heap of ashes and half burnt papers, we could see bank statements, instruction books on home appliances, and greeting cards of their birthdays, Father's Day, and Mother's Day that our parents had saved for years. I remember saying to Sabrina, "This scares me. Why would they burn these things?" We also thought about burglars. We looked into windows to see if we could see anything unusual inside or find any door or window unlocked or broken into.

We did not find any clue as to what was happening there. We were getting more and more uneasy, so we decided to ride into the nearby town in the hope that we might find them there. On the way, we passed the house of Dad's sister and there we saw Dad's truck coming. Turning my car around, we went back and stopped. We were really scared then because we thought that Dad had gone there to confront his sister with the accusations of her husband having an affair with our mother. Needless to say there was no basis for these accusations and Dad had been throwing these at Mother since we were kids. Trying to act natural was hard because this was a place I had not visited in years. Dad asked us what we were doing there and where were we going. We said we had come to have lunch with them. Incidentally, this was not unusual; we occasionally invited ourselves to their home for lunch or dinner. Within a short time, all four of us left to go back to their farm.

Once inside, we prepared sandwiches for lunch. When we sat at the dining table to eat, the silence was very awkward. No one was saying much. Neither Sabrina nor I was able to bring the problem up.

The words would just not come out of our mouths. Finally, all four of us went outside to pick cherries. Dad left after filling a couple of cups. We didn't really know where he had gone.

This gave mother, Sabrina, and me a chance to talk. Mother told us that Dad was talking about divorce. We both told Mother, "If that's what he wants, let him."

We assured her that she would have a home with either of us. Mother did not agree with us about the divorce. She felt it was unfair and she did not deserve to be treated like that after she had given so much to the marriage. She said she had worked very hard to help him accomplish whatever he wanted to get in life. She felt she gave up so much to stay with him and she was not willing to be thrown out now. Mother said, "He is not going to run me off." I did not know whether to support Mother's decision or discourage her from taking a stand like that. I just told Mother if she needed me for anything, she could call me anytime and I would be there for her.

When we returned to the house, Dad was sitting on the porch, still very quiet. Soon, we were leaving.

We were dissatisfied with ourselves that we had done nothing to solve the problem. The next day, Tuesday, neither Sabrina nor I heard anything from them. We wanted to believe that things became better again just as they did other times in the past.

On Wednesday, I went to our Bible Study group. Mother and Dad also used to come to the Bible Study group every Wednesday. Dad did not come that day. However, Mother came along with the neighbors. In the Bible group, our leader asked who all had any requests for special prayers. My mother requested a prayer for Dad. To my surprise, she did not request special prayer for the problem Mother was having with Dad; she asked for a prayer for his safety, instead. She told the group that Dad had had a near accident with the tractor that day. It so happened that their tractor was giving them some problems in getting started. In order to crank the engine, he pushed it to roll down the hill and then tried to climb on it while it was moving. Mother said that he nearly fell in trying to get on the tractor. During the prayer, I took my mother's hand, kissed her on the cheek and told her that I loved her.

After the Bible group, Mother and I did not have a chance to talk to each other. She rode back home with the neighbors while I took a cousin home. Later, I went back to Dad and Mother's. There was very little conversation. I was at a loss; I didn't know what to say. I did tell them that Sabrina was having a cook-out the next night, that was Thursday night, and she would very much like them to come. I explained to them that the fiance' of Sabrina's daughter was coming home after a long time. We all were very fond of him and wanted this gathering in his honor. I asked them to come knowing fully well that there was little hope of their coming. I was afraid that Mother would say, "Oh, I am sorry! But, Dad is not feeling well." This was Mother's pet excuse when Dad was in one of his "moods" and they were supposed to join a dinner or social get together with the relatives or friends: "Roy is sick," or "Roy is not feeling well." However, to my surprise, Dad broke the ice to say they would be there. Dad loved his grandkids. I suppose that Dad didn't want to disappoint his granddaughter on an occasion like this.

As I was getting ready to leave, Mother and Dad asked me to mark my favorite verses and passages in their Bible. I gladly marked my choicest verses and hymns and some which I thought particularly would give them some peace of mind. This gave me some hope that things might get back to normal. We said our good-byes. Dad did not come out to see me up to the car as they both usually did. Mother walked me up to the car and asked me, as she usually did, to call when I reached home. This kept them from worrying about my twelve-mile drive home alone. During that drive home, I sang the Lord's praises and prayed really feeling better about how things turned out that Wednesday evening. When I reached home, I promptly phoned them to convey that I was okay. I did not want them to worry even a little bit about me when they seemed under so much stress.

Thursday afternoon, my husband came in very tired and hungry. Although, a little later, we were going to that cook-out at Sabrina's house, my husband was too hungry to wait and he didn't particularly care about the grilled food. So on our way to Sabrina's house, we stopped at a restaurant where my husband could have some vegetables for supper. From the restaurant we drove to Sabrina's house. As we were nearing her house we saw Dad walking. I realized later that he had come out walking because he wanted to talk to me and he could not have done that in the presence of everyone else.

We stopped and I asked Dad to get in and ride with us. As soon as he got in, he started saying those awful things about Mother. He said if he only knew who the man was who went to bed with her, he would go there and kill him. This was unusual. In the past, Dad has not made these accusations in front of my husband. He went on to say that he could never satisfy her as a man. He said that afternoon he went to the bathroom to find out what she had been up to. He said that he saw that the bathroom floor was sticky. So he went on his knees and smelled the bathroom floor. He was convinced that the floor had the smell of sex. Actually, Mother had cleaned the bathroom and waxed the floor because some house guests were coming that week. Mother explained to him again and again that it was really wax but he was sure in his mind-- although he did not say the word in front of me-- that it was semen. We had heard these accusations from Dad before, but what was unusual about it was the fact that he was saying all those things in front of my husband. In the past, he had been troubled by similar things he imagined about Mother, but no matter how upset he was, he had not made these accusations in the presence of my husband. It was so hard for me to sit there and listen to those things about my own Mother. I could not restrain myself any longer. Finally, I said, "Dad! Mother has not been the type of woman you say she has, and there is no way you can prove your accusations."

He retorted angrily that he did not have to prove it. I tried to reason with him, but he would not listen. He said, "I know this is the fact and no (there is no use) telling me otherwise."

By this time, Sabrina's daughter and her fiance were walking his mother out to her car to leave. We were still in our car discussing what Dad had just said. Sabrina's daughter kept asking us to come on in the house. I asked Dad for us to go in and talk to Sabrina about this, but, he said, "No! I don't want her to know." Then I had to tell him that Sabrina already knew because I had told her and I could not handle it alone.

When he heard this, he began to get out of the car and said, "You girls may hate me and I may go to hell for what I am going to do." With that remark, he began walking away. Sabrina's daughter asked him where was he going and he tersely said, "Home."

Since then, this sentence of Dad's, "You girls may hate me and I may go to hell for what I am going to do," has rung in my ears a thousand times. I have pondered over what it meant to me then and what it means to me now in hindsight. At that time, nothing went through my mind except the divorce. I thought he was telling me that he was going to divorce Mother. The thought of divorce itself was shocking. When Mother told us about it just the day before, it didn't really hit me. But now I was hearing from Dad himself what Mother told us yesterday. I was stunned and don't remember when I went into the house and what I said or did. When Mother was getting ready to leave, I think I hugged her, bade her bye and told her I loved her. Dad did not say anything to me, nor I to him. I sat there for a long time, trying to sort out in my mind what had just taken place.

After the guests were gone and Sabrina had time to sit down with me, we talked with each other about our concerns and thoughts about what we could do in the situation. One idea that we both seemed to like was to seek the help of our pastor. Same Thursday night, though a little late to call anybody, we went ahead anyway and called our pastor. Reverend Somerset had been the pastor at our church for the last several years and was very close to the family. He arrived soon after our call. He had known what was going on because Dad had gone to the pastor and related to him all those accusations against Mother. In hindsight, this again was very unusual for Dad to go to anyone outside the family and complain about it. It seems that Dad was trying desperately to get someone to believe in his accusations. At any rate, this was a shock to the pastor because he didn't have the slightest hint that there was any problem between them. He thought that they were so devoted to each other. The pastor wanted to talk with Mother alone, but Dad would not allow that without he, himself, being present in that meeting. We imagine that Dad did not allow such a meeting in his absence because he was afraid that she might turn the pastor against him. Since Dad was outright against it, the pastor was not able to hear Mother's side.

With the pastor, we discussed how we could get Dad some help. Knowing that he would not willingly accept or reach out for help, we thought that the best step, for sake of Mother and Dad, would be to commit him to a hospital. The thought of committing Dad to a hospital against his will hurt us inside but we knew we had to do something to get help. By this time, it was quite late in the night so we agreed to call our family doctor, first thing in the morning. My husband and I left Sabrina's home sometime after eleven in the night. Returning home, my husband and I discussed again what had taken place in the car earlier that evening. We felt more strongly than ever before that the divorce would be the best thing for Dad and Mother. Personally, I wanted Mother to get out of this relationship and for once just think of her self.

That night was restless, and I certainly dreaded the morning. I got up about seven in the morning, sat up on the side of our bed and shook. It just took me over and I could not control this feeling. My husband asked me what was wrong with me. I told him, "I don't know. I just can't stop shaking. I can't explain this feeling. All I know is that I am not shaking from feeling cold." He offered to stay home and go with us to the doctor to discuss the hospital commitment but I insisted that he go and attend to his work.

A little later, when I talked with Sabrina over the telephone, she too told me about her waking up around five and shaking. We thought then that it was our "nerves" acting up in the knowledge of what we were going to do that morning. Sabrina said she would go to Dad and Mother and try to talk Dad into getting some help. I said it might be better if we went together. She thought Dad might listen to it better if she alone talked to him. It took me a while to get her to see that it would be better for us to approach Dad together. Before we left to see Dad and Mother, we called Dad's doctor. The doctor was not there but I talked with his nurse and told her what was happening. She made an appointment for a later hour that morning, hoping that we could talk Dad into going in to the doctor's clinic. She said if we weren't there by the appointment hour, she would have the doctor call in and he would try talking to Dad.

Around nine that Friday morning, Sabrina and I drove up to Mother and Dad's house. As we drove up to their driveway, Sabrina yelled, "Ashley! look at the front door." The front door's bottom half is solid and the top half is glass. The glass of the front door was shattered and blown out. Fear hit me hard. We could hardly get out of the car. Our legs felt very weak, and while walking our knees were knocking against each other. I didn't know what else we might find. We could feel in the air that something was terribly wrong. It had an uneasy quiet about it. Climbing up those steps, our legs felt so heavy as if somebody had poured lead in them. We could hardly get to the top of the porch. The first thing we saw was Mother sitting in her recliner, her head leaning to one side as if she were asleep. To this day, I thank God that Dad did not destroy Mother's face. She was so beautiful and peaceful. She couldn't have known the fate of her death. The shotgun-blast had entered her abdomen. Her flesh and internal organs lay outside her body. Sitting beyond the shattered door was Dad, his head blown off. Our eyes quickly flashed from his neck to his feet, and we saw the gun braced between his feet and legs and his hands still on the gun. Flesh was on the wall and ceiling, and on the doorway, the bed and the curtains of the adjoining room. His flesh had turned purple and gray. There was a headless person sitting in that chair instead of Dad. We could not bear to look at him again. One look and that was enough to get it permanently embedded in our mind. It was such a horrible sight; we don't know if we can ever erase it from our minds. However, we had to walk past him to get to Mother. It has haunted us ever since then. We did not touch him as there was no doubt in our minds that he was dead. We now regret that we did not touch him as that was the only time we could have. But at that time, it would have been impossible.

There was no doubt in our mind that Dad was dead but I thought Mother might be alive. We touched her and stroked her face but she was already cold. We could not believe this. Sabrina screamed at the top of her voice, "Why daddy, why!" It was horrible. Sabrina and I held each other. We were screaming, going out on the porch and then back in, thinking that surely someone will hear us! Finally Sabrina went on her knees to stop herself from shaking and running in and out to the driveway. The phone was there, near, on the floor, with blood splattered all over it. It seemed too horrible--it couldn't be happening to us. But we were facing a situation that we had to do something about. Somehow, she managed to pick up the receiver and asked, "Who do we call?" All I could think of was the emergency number, 911. The lady on the other end did not understand a word. Sabrina repeated it twice, maybe more. The lady kept on saying, "Now slow down and tell me again." Sabrina kept on saying, "My Mom and Dad are dead. Daddy shot Mother and he shot himself." She finally made them understand who and where we were. At last we had succeeded in calling for help, but then we faced the ordeal of waiting. Sometime later, police began to arrive. The sheriff told us to go out on the porch. We sat on the swing for a minute and then we stood up again. We were pacing the porch as we were not able to sit down. The family doctor called in, as promised, on the dot, at the time which was scheduled for Dad's appointment; but, it was too late now. From the time of seeing the door shattered, to each following scene, we seemed to feel more and more numb. It was almost as if we were in a nightmare, trying to wake up, but were not able to. The fatigue of crying, running and screaming was taking over.

The day was very long-- so much was going on. The sheriff's questions needed to be answered: If we had any idea why Dad would do this?; If he left a note?; If we moved anything? The ambulance crew had to wait for the county coroner, because Dad and Mother could not be moved until he came to pronounce them dead. We were told that the coroner has to satisfy himself that it was indeed a case of murder and suicide and all questions and doubts are satisfactorily answered. At any rate the county coroner determined that Mother and Dad died the night before, only a couple of hours after they left us at Sabrina's house. Dad first shot her twice and then he shot himself in the head. The sheriff asked us if we thought otherwise. We told him that we did not think any different since it was so obvious that Dad had killed Mother and then himself.

TV stations and newspaper reporters were swarming around, asking all kind of questions which made us mad. We asked the police to make the newspapers and TV people leave the property. The TV crews got their shots from the end of the driveway, not being allowed to come on the property.

The sheriff's office advised us to move all the furniture from the house and not leave anything there that we would not want stolen. They told us that rogues were known to go to a place of crime and haul off stuff knowing that no one would be there to watch. Hearing this, family and neighbors were moving furniture, cleaning up the chairs, walls, the floor, and tearing out the carpet to remove blood and body tissues. Our minds could not accept what was happening. We felt as if it were happening far away somewhere else, or like we were watching a film. We were there and yet we were not there. But some inner strength was holding us, carrying us through. The Lord was our inner strength.

Things were moving so fast around us, whirling and swarming. So many questions were being asked to us, and so many questions we were asking ourselves. We wanted some answers too, but where would we get them?

AFTERMATH AND THE HEALING OF WOUNDS

The night of that doomsday and the following days, our minds and bodies seemed to be floating and we did not have any control over keeping ourselves tied to the ground. We were in shock and just couldn't believe that it had really happened. Sometimes we felt we were in a bad dream, and when we woke up we would find out that what we were seeing was not true. Sometimes, it felt as if the body was not there. At times, the body felt completely empty and the soul and spirit were floating around, looking in, searching for Mother and Dad. We were like the kids, playing hide and seek, but we couldn't find the ones we were seeking.

The funeral home was crowded and there were people everywhere. The numb feeling continued as we spoke to the visitors at the funeral home; we did not really know or remember what they said or even who was there. We barely existed through the funeral because we were still in shock. We were there for people to see us, but we were hardly mentally present.

Most of our relatives were there to stand by us and to help. Our friends prepared meals for our families in the local churches and brought them to us at meal times. We were shown lots of love and given assurances by friends and relatives that they would be close to us at a time like this. But how long can people stay with the survivors, even if they wanted to. After Mother and Dad were laid to rest, people began to leave one by one.

The state of shock continued for several weeks. Our minds and bodies continued to be numb during this time. We were having flashbacks of the scene of our parents' deaths flashing in front of our eyes hundreds of times a day. Every time we closed our eyes, we could see the flashbacks. It was awful, we could see and hear everything of that morning, including the smell of the blood. If we sat still for a minute, we would have the flashbacks. We could not sleep without waking up several times. Most times, the nightmares of their deaths woke us up. In the dreams or in half sleep, all we could see was Mother's and Dad's dead bodies, the sight of blood, Dad's head blown away, and the flesh all over the place. Ashley even went over and over the scene we saw, trying to figure out exactly how that final event took place.

In order to sense that event completely, she even imagined herself in Mother's body, and feeling the impact of those two shotgun blasts. As a result of imagining this, her body would become limp and lifeless. Ashley would then picture Dad, having fired at Mother twice, trying to sit in his recliner, positioning the gun at his own self, but not getting the aim right. She would imagine the gun slipping away, and the shot going through the wall instead of hitting him. Incidentally, according to the coroner's report, two shots were fired at Mother which killed her. The third shot hit the wall and the fourth killed Dad. Ashley would then imagine Dad going to his rocker, holding the shotgun between his feet, pushing the trigger and POW!. We were exhausted in trying to imagine exactly how it happened. There were questions that we never ceased to ask ourselves: Did Mother ever realize that Dad was shooting at her? What did Mother and Dad talk about on their way home, that last day when we saw them? Did Mother experience any pain? We do not have any answers to these questions and it makes us mad that we will never find out what happened and how it happened. But the pictures of what we saw that morning, and what we imagined about how it happened haunted us so much that we didn't want to go to bed. Being awake was no better either, since we were not able to control our thoughts about their deaths. The scenes of what we saw were consuming our minds entirely.

We asked the Lord to help us keep our trust in him. Our throats were sore from crying. We could hardly speak because the sounds would not come out of our throats. We just wanted God to take away our pain and sorrow. We wanted to feel his presence near. But, our souls weakened by intense grief were not capable of feeling His presence. We struggled with the question of why Dad did this to us and what could we have done to avoid the deaths of our parents. We were infested with doubts and admonitions. However, just when we thought we were going to break down and didn't have the strength to fight the grief, flashbacks, and nightmares, we got that strength to go on from some source unbeknown to us. We believe that guidance and strength came from God.

We do not know whether people feel uncomfortable in facing us or they don't know what to say or do, but the fact is that with the exception of a few, we have not seen much of our friends or relatives after the funeral day. This also happened after the death of our brother, Brian, who, as we mentioned earlier, committed suicide in the prime of his life. At that time, the few friends who did visit us didn't come back after we tried to talk to them about our brother's death. It seems that the subject of death makes people uncomfortable. If you ignore that message and still talk about it, people might want to keep you at arm's length. The experience after our brother's death had made us wiser, so we tried not to make the same mistake again. However, after Mother and Dad's deaths, many people didn't come to visit us, even though we had not talked about this subject. At times, we felt people were avoiding us as if we had the plague. The only exceptions were Mother's sisters, who stood by us and cried and grieved with us. In the first few months, we wondered whether people were scared of us thinking that we might be mentally unstable, or if they were afraid that there may be something seriously wrong with our family for three people to die under unnatural circumstances. Were they afraid of getting involved, in case we too would lose control and kill ourselves? Some even told us they believed that suicidal tendencies are hereditary. What a great help that was! That just tapped on our worst fears.

At that time we were struggling with the same question, hoping that someone would tell us suicide was not written in one's genes. People don't have to say something just for the sake of talking when they visit a person in grief. It may be better to be silent and just sit there. Just being there with a person in grief can make all the difference when one is feeling totally alone. Even if it does not bring comfort right away, at least one is not hurting a survivor by saying the wrong thing. One, who has not lost a loved one, cannot realize what it means to grieve. Until we experienced the grief ourselves, we didn't know what one really felt in the grief. We would rather have had people come and say nothing. If we needed to talk, we would have liked someone to sense that need at that moment and encourage us to talk then. That would have assured us that we had a friend and he or she really cared. See! One doesn't have to know the "right" thing to say. There is no right thing that needs to be said.

To avoid embarrassment to our friends and relatives, we found ourselves telling strangers what had happened. Some told us that they remembered having read it in the newspapers. Our talking sometimes seemed to make some people uncomfortable, but most of them listened and were very sympathetic. The thought of them never coming back and not seeing us again did not hurt us; it wasn't a friend or another family member turning their back on us.

If we didn't believe in God and weren't able to feel his presence and receive strength from Him, we could have easily wallowed in grief. Even with our faith in God, it had been so hard. We had been lonely and felt the empty times, especially the Sundays, holidays, and birthdays when we always got together with them. Those were special times for us as a family. Now, we spent many of these special days by ourselves so we wouldn't remember all the time how it used to be.

We were asking hundreds of questions over and over again, in our minds, to Mother and Dad: "Mother, why did you go on putting up with Dad, why didn't you leave?" "Dad why did you also have to take Mother with you?"; "Dad! if you loved us so much as you said you did, then why did you have to hurt us like this? There was no end to our questions. In our minds, we were telling them things we wished we had told them when they were living, things we wanted to do for them to make their lives more enjoyable. We wished Mother had got out more and enjoyed life for her sake.

At one point, our counselor suggested that each one of us sit down and write a letter to Mother and Dad, and say all the things we wanted to say. At first, we could not imagine writing to our dead parents. We also shuddered at the idea of writing to them because we were afraid we might not be able to stop crying. However, we overcame all those fears to sit down and write.

This is the letter that Ashley wrote:

> Dearest Mother and Dad,
>
> There is so much emptiness in my life since you've been gone. My Sunday afternoons and Wednesday evenings after church will never be the same. We spent Sunday afternoons together just sitting and talking, sometimes napping, but always in one another's presence. That meant so much to me because I loved you. Each time we left, we always exchanged a hug and a kiss, and Dad, you would always say, "I am not going to let you go" and then we would exchange our "I- love- you" with you and Mother. Then, Mother would most likely walk to the porch with us and wait until my husband and I drove down the drive, then wave another bye.
>
> Things just aren't that way anymore since that morning when Sabrina and I came to try and help you Dad! We knew you were very depressed and troubled, but never, never, did I want to believe you would kill Mother, and then yourself. Dad, you know how you and Mother grieved when your only son, Brian, shot and killed himself. Dad, first, all those hours, months, and then years, we cried and asked ourselves, "Why?" (after Brian's suicide). Now, Sabrina and I, all the grandchildren, our husbands, your son's wife, your family, and Mother's family are asking again, "Why." Why couldn't we have helped you? Dad why did you have to take Mother? You left us so alone, so hurt. I bet you never thought that Sabrina and I would be the ones to find you. That terrible sight as we stepped upon the porch and through the shattered door, we saw you both dead.
>
> Dad, I know you couldn't have been yourself, some evil, sick mind was within you. You always said, "I love you more than you'll ever know." Our Dad would not have hurt us this way.
>
> Dad, I could never believe the accusations you made against our sweet, gentle, and loving mother. If she was like what you said all those years, we would have seen and heard about it.

But you know Mother did not drive, so, she didn't get to go anywhere unless you took her.

Very few places, she went without you. When we were kids, she always had farming chores to do, plus her housework, cooking, and sewing our clothes. When did she ever have time or a chance to go for another man. Mama and Papa lived right across the road, and kept watch and reported to you every day. That's where you always went first, you didn't come to see us first.

Mother, you know I stuck by you in Arizona when you and Dad separated. I came back to Georgia with you. That four day bus drive was horrible. How happy we were to stop off in Rome, Ga. Little did we know at that moment how much we would miss Dad, Sabrina, and our brother Brian in the weeks and months to come. Sabrina had already set a date with her fiance for their marriage before you and I left. They married soon after we left Arizona. We could not be present at the wedding.

I can remember so well our aunt, your sister, coming to the house where I was spending the night with another aunt, very early in the morning. It scared me at first, but, when she said, my daddy and Brian were there, I thought my world was back together again. Then we all lived together. Things went well for a while, then the fussing started again. Mother, I remember you ironing clothes and doing the housework for the neighbors to help with the bills. How hard you worked Mother and I wasn't a lot of help to you at that time. I am ashamed now as I look back.

Sabrina and I had just recently said you and Dad could still work circles around us. You still could spend the day working in the hot sun, never complaining, feeling happy while doing it. Each year, you would say you were not having as large a garden as last year, but as you started to till the soil and plant, the garden would turn out to be as large as ever. Neither you nor Mother could sit and be idle.

Dad, you broke yourself down at an early age, working so hard. You probably had no choice, and through the years never knew when to quit.

I hope you both know how much I loved you. I hope neither of you died thinking that we had turned against you, and that you had no one on your side.

Mother, the day of that awful, awful morning, I can still see the look on your face as if you had just fallen asleep. You must not have known that Dad walked out of the bedroom with that shotgun pointed at you. I pray that you didn't suffer, Mother. The coroner said you died instantly. I don't think God would have let you suffer, Mother. He was with you and I know you have sweet peace now.

I do wonder what Dad did after he killed you, Mother. Did he hurt knowing what he did? Did he cry? Did he touch you? Did he pray to God? Did he think anything at all? How long did he wait before sitting in the rocker, putting the shotgun between his feet and pulling the trigger on himself? I know that you died instantly Dad, and I pray that you found peace with God.

I believe within my heart that you've been reunited with my brother, Brian, in heaven. Sabrina and I were supposed to have you for only a short while. Now, we, who are left here, have to be strong. We have to do the best we can; God will continue to carry us and give us the strength for each tomorrow.

Even as we sort your personal things, I wonder what we are doing. Even now, I don't want to believe that you are dead. I want to believe that you will be back, and then I ask myself, " Why are we taking their belongings." Mother and Dad! I picked up each of your's bed pillows, held them and could smell where you had once laid your heads. Sabrina and I plan to let that be the last thing we remove and wash.

Oh, yes! Rover (parents' dog) sure is lost, without you being there to take care of him. He misses you and is also grieving your absence. We've tried to talk to him, explain to him what had happened and tell him that you wouldn't be back, but how much can a dog understand. He looks so sad and the way he cries when he sees us, maybe he understands more than we think.

We are going to try to sell the farm as soon as we get your house fixed up. We would have liked to save the house. There is just no possible way for us to keep it and settle your estate. Dad, Brian's son is going to take your truck. His college is very far away. He has to travel a long distance when he comes home to spend the weekend. He is just not dependable for such long drive with the car he is driving now. You know how you worried about his having trouble on the road.

Dad, Father's day is next Sunday and today I found a card I had given you on a previous Father's day. You told me on Wednesday before you died that you had been reading a card I gave you. Well, I found the one that was on your desk. In the card, I had written, "I hope you can be as proud to say that I'm your daughter as I am to say, you're my Dad." And then, I had written a poem which had the lines:

I know our bond will always last.
A special man, so wise and strong,
I'll love you Dad, all life long."

Dad I did love you all life long, and I still love you after your life is gone. I'll hold on to the good memories of both, you and mother. I know you loved each other, and I guess, I'll always ask, "Why did you do it?"

Love, Your Baby,
Ashley.

Just about that time, this is the letter that Sabrina wrote to her deceased parents:

Dear Mother and Dad,
It is hard for me at this time to write to you. I miss you both so much. It's hard to realize that you're gone. I want to wake up and find out this was just a terrible dream.

I want to tell you how much I love you. One thing that we didn't do often enough was to express our love for each other. I wish you were here, so I could hug you. I had no idea on Thursday night what was going to happen next, when I hugged you and told you how much I loved you. Mother, you told me that day that you loved me, and I too told you the same. Dad you told me you loved me more than I would ever know and then you said bye like a final bye. I said, I'll see you on Sunday and you didn't respond. I didn't understand then what it all meant. I wish I had said something that would have made a difference in what happened later. I wish I could have stopped it.

Daddy, Ashley and I were coming to talk to you that morning to try to get you some help. Why didn't you give us a chance? Daddy, I never would have thought that you would put us through this again after what we had gone through with Brian's death. You said that you loved us, then how could you do what you did? Dad, if you only knew how much pain and heartache we are having, you wouldn't have done this to us.

I miss you both so much. I don't want to say bye to you, because I still want you to be here. But deep down in my heart, I know you cannot be here, ever. But Mother, I do believe that now you are with Brian in heaven. Daddy, only the Lord knows if you're in heaven.

I believe it will be beautiful in heaven with no troubles and no heartaches. Mother and Dad, I miss you here on earth. But I know you will be happy there. You will have love and happiness.

Mom, here is something you would have liked to say. It is written by Carol Mirkel. The name of the poem is "After Glow." Here it is:

I'd like the memory of me to be a happy one,
I'd like to leave an afterglow of smiles when life is done.
I'd like to leave an echo whispering softly down the ways,
Of happy times, and laughing times, and bright and sunny days.
I'd like the tears of those who grieve, to dry before the sun,
Of happy memories that I leave when life is done.

Love, your daughter
Sabrina.

Although we couldn't imagine ourselves writing these letters, once we began, it was easy. We could put on paper our worst hurt, the pain of their absence, and the loneliness we felt. As we remembered the special occasions, the happy ones, and the sad ones, we could still feel the bond we had with them. Writing these letters, we experienced the mixture of love, anger, hate, and hurt. We also experienced the heartbreak of never being able again to embrace or tell Mother and Dad how much we loved them. We felt thankful to God that our parents knew we loved them. They sure knew because we told them so often. We did not feel any guilt on that account, but we felt guilty for not knowing and not doing something to stop this senseless act that has changed our lives so drastically. We read out loud what we had written in the letters; it was as if we had talked to Dad and Mother. But as we did so, we were sobbing. We still had no answers, and we realized there would never be. However, writing a letter helped us, as we could never say some of those things to Dad's face.

As the shock and numbness wore off, on occasions, we began to feel very angry with Dad for causing this hurt and taking Mother away with him. In the counseling, we began to learn about Dad's illness and to sense how much he was troubled from the inside. Later, along with the periods of anger, we began to feel forgiveness and compassion for Dad. A letter written by Sabrina at the point of this new understanding and compassion is here:

> *Dear Daddy,*
> *I can hear you say, "What about me?" Yes, Daddy, you do deserve some happiness too. You didn't have a brother or a sister here that loved you. Daddy, you didn't have a family except one sister who really cared about you. Your family was more interested in what you could do for them. And after that, they would hurt you every chance they got.*
> *Daddy, now you know the only ones that really cared about you and loved you were the Lord, Mother, and your children. The Lord and Mother were by your side all of your life. You and Mother worked side by side for the entire time of your life. Daddy, you worked yourself to death because you thought it would pay off one day and the farm would be yours. Yes, you deserved it because you paid for it all your life. Daddy, you had so much love for your parents, brothers, and sisters. For you, they could do no wrong. I hope in the Lord's eye you deserve to be in heaven. Daddy, I still don't like what you did to our Mother. I can't understand why we lacked communication, why we couldn't talk it out.*
> *Daddy, I loved you. I hope you knew that I would miss you,*
>
> *Love, your daughter,*
> *Sabrina.*

We feel that we have come a long way in our recovery from the grief of our parents' loss. We still have bad days, but the number of such days is reducing. All holidays, birthdays, Mother's and Father's days are still difficult but getting easier than the previous ones. The sight of Mother and Dad that morning was causing a lot of turmoil in our minds. So our counselor helped us to go through the whole series of events of that morning in our minds. This time, we were to repeat these events with a relaxed body and mind, unlike the first time when we were hooping, hollering, and panicking. We tried hard to stop the flashbacks by telling ourselves to stop them. The more we tried, the more we realized we couldn't. To get rid of the flashbacks which were happening by dozens a day, our counselor suggested that since we couldn't stop them we should change the content of the flashbacks. In the flashbacks, we were seeing the bodies of our parents on chairs, the blood-splattered carpet, pieces of body tissues and bone fragments on the walls and ceilings. Along with seeing these scenes, we could even smell the blood just as we smelled that morning.

These flashbacks were tormenting our minds. Our counselor suggested that we prepare a scene of our choice. He asked us to think of a pleasant place where we wanted to be now. He encouraged us to imagine the ocean, mountains, blue sky during the Spring or the Fall. He said any season other than when it actually happened, and to imagine smelling the flowers that we loved most. He let us imagine these scenes in great details and practice this over and over again until we got it down pat. Then he asked us to imagine this scene very fast as if we were seeing it on a fast run video. Once we got good at it, we were asked to throw our own "counter flashback" on the real flashbacks. We would close our eyes, feel the ocean breeze touching our skin and flowing through our hair, and we would even succeed in smelling the fragrance of roses. Sometimes, to increase the soothing effect of the counter flashbacks, we would hear someone singing our favorite verses in the background. This helped us to get a handle on our flashbacks.

Thinking about ways in which counseling helped us, we greatly appreciate the help in opening up and talking about our innermost feelings, good or bad, and not to be ashamed of crying. There were things we could not tell our own families, lest we disturb them more; we could talk to the counselor without worrying about whether or not this was going to upset him.

During this period, we have been able to talk about our lives from childhood, remembering things we had locked deep inside our minds, trying to see how and why our families were so unhappy. We experienced various stages of anger and blame; anger and blame going around and around, sometimes pointed at one parent, or both parents, or at our own selves, or particular relatives and friends. We realized that some things were not anybody's fault although they appeared as if they were. Some things just could not be any other way. With Dad's jealousy and Mother's determination not to leave him, there were not many options available. We did not know the true intentions of Dad. We wished that we had gotten help earlier. We wished that we had known about Dad's problem as we know it now. Anyway, we are not spending that much energy on anger and blame, now.

At one stage, each one of us felt so much hate and anger at Dad. Our counselor used the empty chair. We would talk to that chair as if Dad were sitting there. It first seemed too much of a make believe game and kid-stuff, but it got rid of so much of our anger, and then we also began to see things from Dad's side. Now, we understand that our Dad had an illness, and he could not see and reason things as we expect of people normally. We know that our Mother lived a life that could not be faulted. She devoted her entire life to him, and was completely loyal and faithful to him but because of his illness, his unreal suspicions, he could not see that. With these thoughts, we vary between anger and forgiveness towards our father. Our counselor keeps reminding us to think of something pleasant and comforting, when we relive the horrible scene of finding Dad and Mother dead. But those scenes are now fewer and farther between. We still miss our parents a lot, but when we are sad, we try to think of the pleasant times we had with both of them. Sometimes, we think or dream about them being turned away from us or being upset and angry with us. Then we have to tell ourselves, that we did the best we could, although we wished we could have done better. We still miss them very much. However, a large part of the time, we can remember them without crying, and without the feelings of guilt, blame and anger.

MY HUSBAND

Austin had a disorder of jealousy. He was morbidly jealous of relatives, friends, and strangers alike. He had periods of "darkness," that is, the periods of depression, long before he met his wife. At first, suspicions and accusations regarding his wife's unfaithfulness surfaced during these periods of darkness, later, they became part of their everyday life. Austin's abuse of substance added fuel to the fires of jealousy until there were no periods free of the rage and the fear.

Austin was a study of contradictions: a very kind man and yet so callous; full of humor and fun but equally full of bitterness and rage; fearless, bold and adventurous, yet too fearful to trust anybody; he was outwardly a normal, happy-go-lucky guy, but inside, severely sick with a mental disorder of jealousy.

Holly, wife of Austin, for most of the twenty-one years of marriage, rode with her husband on his emotional roller coaster, sometimes, trying to adapt to it, at other times, to stick with him in "health and sickness." She tried hard to change him and to take help for both, for him and herself. During this period, she left him several times and came back to him, for her love and compassion for him, and at times, for the sake of the children; an experience that all women, in a similar situation, will identify with. In the final phase, she faced fear almost on a daily basis; she took the beatings from him and fought back. This is a story of a woman who is more courageous than most of us. She tried to the very last to get him help. When she had tried everything she could think of and she became convinced that he would not help himself or accept help from others, she decided to leave him. This decision was different from all the previous decisions she had taken. This time she had seen clearly that her children were hurting emotionally and he was emotionally abusing one of the children. Once she became convinced that it was detrimental to the children, she acted decisively and then there was no going back on her decision. Ironically, the firmness of her decision and the irrevocability of it, led to his suicide. Had she known what was really the nature of his disorder, and if the appropriate interventions were available to them, we tend to think that their lives would have followed a different course.

Within the six months of their dating, he had told her, "Now that I have found you, I will never let you go." He never did, as long as he was alive!

Such is the extent of desperation. Such is the need for control and possession in an untreated disorder of jealousy. Here is the story, MY HUSBAND, in Holly's own words.

If it were possible for me to carry this story to my grave silently, I would. But too many people have been carried silently to their graves with this secret buried in their hearts. I cannot be silent. This secret is about a monster. The name of the monster is "insane jealousy." It commits its atrocities in the name of love. I have faced this monster in combat many times. In our final conflict, it assumed the face of death. A death which I narrowly escaped; a death my husband did not. Prior to this, I spent many years of my life living in a combat zone, struggling for my life, surviving one day at a time.

I am not a masochist. I am not a statistic of domestic violence. I did not stay in this relationship because, in some sick way, I needed this pain. He was sick. He had a disease which is the malignancy of marriage. A disease which is not yet understood by society and the mental health professionals. I am convinced that insane jealousy is widely responsible for spousal abuse. I could be the woman you have seen, in the work place, with the black eye, bruises on her arms, her face sketched with fear, dark circles, and swollen eyes from crying and sleeplessness. I could be your daughter or your sister. I do not wish to be identified; instead that my voice be heard.

As I sit alone and write this, I think of the years I struggled alone with this disease. I think of the books I have read in my quest for answers. I think of the nights I stayed awake alone and searched my mind for answers. I think of my life's journey through the wilderness, which was my marriage, and my struggle to educate myself and change things for my family. The disease of jealousy, by its very nature, is conducive to silence and shame. It manifests itself in the most primitive and vulnerable area of a couple's life, their sexual relationship, and gradually but unrelentingly, affects every aspect of the lives of the victims. As a consequence, each family member is affected by its dark shadow. I will its silence broken.

Women, who become involved with abusive men, had a troubled relationship with the dominant male of their childhood. This was true in my case. My father was a manic depressive. At times, ebullient, at times, depressed to the point of being suicidal, he attempted to compensate for this through work. The son of a widow, being a person of responsibility and honesty, his sole definition of a father was to be a good provider. He was a brilliant man, blonde and handsome, utterly charming at one time, filled with inexplicable rage at another. He was totally inaccessible to me. There was little time and emotional energy left for the fifth daughter born to a man who wanted sons. Although he withheld himself emotionally, he taught me loyalty, determination, and perseverance. Through his towering rages, his larger than life personality, I was exposed to some aspects of an emotional disorder. He also taught me to be complaisant and assume that love, rage, and fear were naturally together. I thought if you love somebody, you will also see their rage, and you must also fear them.

I often felt that my gender was a great disappointment to my father. If only I'd been a boy, I felt I might have been loved. My father was also at his brightest and most personable self when he was around other men. He was a "man's man" who took great pride in his maleness and strength. Ours was a strict and severe environment. Talking was not permitted at the dinner table. Once, when I was very young, I got the giggles at the table. I was told to go outside the house and run around the house. I was terrified of the dark and huddled behind the lamppost at the door waiting until I felt I could go back in.

My mother made up for my father. In her quiet and unassuming way, she was the cement which bonded the family together. She was part American Indian. She had the quiet, stoic grace that many minority women develop. She fully embraced a fundamental Christian religion. A deeply spiritual person, it was difficult for her to separate herself from her religious convictions. She embodied the Judeo-Christian philosophy. Her life's objective was the afterlife. To this end, she made sure we absorbed the great moral principles of the Bible. Any difficulty that life presented her was met with unshakeable conviction that one day it would be overcome and understood. She had absolute faith in the goodness of her children and her husband. Any difficulty that she had with father's emotional problems, she kept to herself. She was fearless in the face of his rages and immovable in dealing with his manipulations. She did what she felt was the right thing. She was a nurturing person who loved life, loved her children, and loved the beauty in the world. She was active in the community and was dependable for helping others in need.

Overworked and involved with family problems, she was unable to see that her youngest daughter was growing up with a distorted sense of self. I felt overshadowed by my siblings. There was the daddy's girl, my sister who was like him in stamina and temperament, the genius with the perfect manners. Another sister, an artist, who was like my mother in temperament and strength, the cheerleader; I the shy and sensitive one. Each one of my siblings were par excellence in some area, an excellence that I was lacking. If I made A's on my report card, I had an elder sister who was allowed to skip a grade because of her superior ability. I was the tag-along. The one who wasn't quite old enough, fast enough or good enough to keep up. In retrospect, I can see the distortion that I experienced. My personality and identity were overshadowed. I was called by my older sister's name so often that I finally got used to it.

My birth order also dictated me to be the odd person out. There were two pairs of my sisters and then I by myself. There was also a large age disparity between me and them, so developmentally, I was too far behind to be part of their group. Left to myself, I learned to think independently, rely on my resources, and push myself to achieve. I spent a great deal of time in solitude, often without my mother's knowing where I was. I felt secure in the rural area and would just go off by myself. Cinderella was my childhood favorite. Fantasy was another defense I developed. I would fantasize that things would somehow magically improve. I read books to escape my loneliness.

My mother was a firm disciplinarian. To her, self- control was an essential goal to be attained. Eager to please her, I struggled for mastery over my temper, which was considerable. I longed to be like her: strong, wise, and capable. Outwardly, I was a good child, I learned my Bible verses, did my chores, controlled my temper, made straight A's in school, and worked very hard to earn Father's love and Mother's approval. Inwardly, I felt I was a just a very plain girl, the one who had a big nose and crooked teeth and who could never catch up with her brilliant and talented sisters. All this transpired before I reached adolescence.

Then we left the farm and moved to a city. Gone were my beloved woods, gone was my favorite aunt who had always made time for the lonely little girl. I changed to four new schools in three years. And adolescence descended with a fury. Turmoil! I had never known such turmoil. Of course my feelings of isolation and loneliness increased. But suddenly my face has grown to my nose! My body changed visibly, and to my surprise I began to be considered pretty. People began to remember my name. Frequent school changes had increased my shyness and defensiveness. I had cultivated the attitude that it didn't really matter what others thought of me. I was unconventional, individualistic and aloof; traits not conducive to building good relationships with my peers.

I had grown from a sad little girl to a sad big girl. The frustration of it all made me angry. I dismissed my father and began to dream of the day when I was an adult with my own family and lived "happily ever after."

Despite my anger and bravado that it didn't matter, the need for love grew even stronger. I was lonely, vulnerable, and naive. The desire to be loved found its outlet in sexual expression. I was sixteen years old and I so much wanted to be loved and accepted by someone. Such a basic human need love is and such a misuse and distortion of sex it can cause.

It lasted six months. My conscience was overwhelmed and I was feeling more damaged. I felt very guilty and confided in no one. I felt that my mother would be irreparably disappointed in me if she knew.

Then he entered my life. From the beginning, there was a great attraction. Austin was everything I desired in a young man. He was handsome, intelligent, marvelously funny, and he wanted me. We quickly became inseparable. I no longer felt the acute loneliness. He seemed perfect. I remembered the adage, "Beware when something is perfect"; but with the recklessness of youth, I threw caution to the wind. I was seventeen, then. However, looking back, I can see there were indications that all was not well. One such indicator was the sheer intensity of his emotions. At the time, I interpreted this as his love for me. He would tell me, "Now that I have found you, I will never let you go." I did not see this as his passion for possession, I saw this as his committed love for me.

He also was insistent on sexual intimacy very early in the relationship. Due to my bad experience earlier, I was hesitant. This was countered with insistence. My resistance was made light of in a coercive, and in retrospect, a manipulative way. But Prince Charming is never manipulative, so I did not allow myself to see him in that light. He was jealous of me and I was jealous of him. He was jealous of my former lover. He had questioned my previous sexual activity and had animosity toward this person. He told me that I was the object of the locker room discussion! This was my first indicator of his morbid jealousy but I did not recognize it then. I was jealous because he made an attempt to initiate another relationship with another young woman while we were actively dating. I did not perceive his jealousy as a problem since I myself felt the same emotion. Now I know there was a very big difference in his jealousy and mine.

We had been constantly together for over a year when I first saw the other part of him, only a glimmer, but the most prophetic of it all. I had not heard from him for several days. I was emotionally very invested in him, therefore, very concerned. When he did agree to see me, it was a person that I had never seen before. Eerie, quiet, subdued, unreachable, he was looking at me strangely with coldness in his eyes. I kept asking him what was wrong. He finally told me that he had been in a bad mood. Then he told me that he would have "times of darkness, blackness." I was a bit shaken by that, but I rationalized it away. After all, I was no stranger to moodiness. I thought something had happened that was causing him a problem and he might be just preoccupied with it. I was not to see or hear about such a mood for several years.

Shortly after this incident, I found out I was pregnant. The only thing for us to do was to marry. We were in love, after all. We had our future to build together. I was confident that we could build a wonderful life together. I was happy and I thought he was happy. Shortly after the marriage, I miscarried. I was devastated. He was very supportive in those times. I thought he was working very hard to be a man, a wage earner and the supporter of the family.

It was critically important that he provide a sound financial base for the family. We moved a number of times, mostly gravitating towards the cities where he felt he could be a better provider. Our first move was 500 hundred miles away. When I learned about it, I did not feel it was in our best interest and felt angry that he reached this decision without consulting me. There was nothing I could do about it. When his mind was made up about something there would be no argument. So in pursuit of my joyous future, I followed.

I had mixed emotions about being there. I was dreadfully homesick, yet, it was an exciting time in my life. We both had good jobs. There was money for entertaining, for cultural events, to enjoy each other, and to grow in our knowledge of each other. It was a time of celebration of love and youth.

Such times were meant to be short lived. We had not yet been married a year when he calmly announced, "I was with a prostitute last night." I was heart broken. I was furious. Crying, and in screaming rage, I asked him why he violated our relationship in that way. He told me it was because he was a virgin the first time we had been together. It had bothered him deeply that I was not, and he wanted to know just what he had missed. It was his first infidelity to me and he promised that it would be his last. Austin had felt justified in what I felt to be a degradation. However, I was damaged goods in my own eyes. How could I expect him to think better of me than I did of myself? That was his first power play on my guilt, but not the last.

Three weeks later, his father died. He was emotionally devastated. I felt so sorry for him. Although, I was still seething over his betrayal, I decided to put those feelings behind me and be strong for him in the face of his loss.

We returned home. It was a difficult transition for him because he was unable to get a good-paying job. Deep in mourning for his father, he began to use marijuana and to move into the drug culture. He was drinking and leaving me at home more and more. I consoled myself, thinking that he wasn't himself and that given some time for healing, things would get better for us again. But they did not.

Our personal interaction was not going smoothly. He would make plans without consulting me and pursue them with determination, in spite of my opposition. Once he took all our savings, of which I had been the primary contributor, and bought a motorcycle. He had to be the dominant one, the "man of the house." There was an inequality that I railed against.

He began to act irresponsibly. There would be interpersonal problems at work, and he would quit, walk out. We began to have financial problems. Our car was repossessed. I began to have very serious thoughts about the continuance of our marriage. I was beginning to feel like I had made a serious mistake.

After two years of marriage, his jealousy became worse. I was very open with him about people who were part of my everyday life, such as the male and female friends, people that I worked with. If, for example, a co-worker told me a joke or a funny anecdote, I would repeat it to my husband. If it were a man who told me, he would question me about this man. If I developed even a casual work relationship with a man, I would be questioned and accused. One night after repeating a story a man had told me, he accused me of sexually wanting to be with this man, in a physically violent way. He grabbed my clothes and pulled me up to his face, while saying this. I slapped him for what I considered to be a slur against me and he shook me hard. This was the first episode of violence. He began to accuse me of wanting to be with other men. This would infuriate me, and I would deny any part of it. I refused to cut myself off from half of the world's population because he was jealous. I knew in my heart that I was innocent of any wrongdoing. Yet he wouldn't apologize for saying those things; he would just act like it hadn't happened.

I had another miscarriage. He confessed another extra-marital affair which had run for several months. When he told me about this woman, I told him I felt like he was morally lacking. I said that was why he was so unreasonably jealous of me, because he was incapable of being faithful. I told him that he was judging me by the faults of his own behavior. I broke down. I returned to my parents' home. Our bright future that I had visualized lay in pieces at my feet.

I began to try to pick up the pieces of my life. I felt like such a failure. I had experienced the freedom of an adult and now was returning in defeat. The atmosphere at home had not changed. My father was still oppressive. My mother was still wonderful, but I felt unable to really communicate with her. I still desperately loved Austin and needed him. I cried a lot in those days. My husband was still calling, coming and seeing me at work. He would apologize for the infidelity and promise to change. I think I wanted my mother to fight for me, or to let me know that I was worth fighting for. But it wasn't that way. Maybe she trusted me to find my own solutions.

There was an alienation that occurred within my family. They did love me but I was caught up in a destructive relationship that was beyond their understanding. They could not really help me and I'm sure they were really frustrated.

I still felt bonded to my husband. The religious principles that had been so firmly instilled in my upbringing would not let me accept the idea of divorcing him. I had taken an oath before God that bound me to him. It didn't occur to me that even Jesus Christ considered adultery grounds for a divorce. After a lot of struggle with myself, I filed for divorce. He was still calling me. *Need* was calling another *need*. I went back to him.

There is no question that at this point in my life I was not a healthy person. I was seeking an affirmation of my self-worth through a sexual relationship with him. I had not yet learned the way to love and accept myself, to stand on my merit, to accept the bad along with the good in me, to forgive my mistakes, and to nurture myself. I had a low self-esteem. I was 22 by now. I was still shy, self-conscious, and lacking in confidence.

Things were better for a while. Then his infidelities began again. They were justified in his eyes because I had been sexually active while we were separated. Again, it was my fault. He became more deeply involved in substance abuse, spending more time away from me. But I was still critically important to him, and growing more so. I now feel that these infidelities were the beginning of a pattern of domination by him that became so firmly entrenched in later years.

My mother developed cancer. Her prognosis was not good. She died during my third pregnancy. Miraculously, I carried this pregnancy to term. He was not supportive of me during this bereavement. I had my child. I could see my mother in her and felt a sense of completeness and love as many women do, who have problems with self-esteem. At last I felt truly capable and whole at least in this area of my life. I was responsible for this little symbol of humanity and I was determined to be a good mother.

It also seemed to bring about a change in my husband. He loved our daughter. His first words to me after her birth were, "Thank you." He was enchanted with Lee and renewed his ambition to be a good provider by working hard. He was very helpful in caring for her; and seemed to be more responsive to my emotional needs, at times. The infidelities and recriminations had ceased but the substance abuse was escalating. He was using hallucinogens, cocaine, angel dust, tranquilizers, and amphetamines.

One night, we had an argument. Lightning fast, he punched a hole in the wall. I was very angry, but also a little frightened, because I knew that his violence was directed at me. But I attributed it to the substance abuse. I told him that I wouldn't allow him to be around our daughter while under any drug's influence. He began to spend more time away from us pursuing the partying life-style.

Two years later, we had an unplanned baby. Austin was ecstatic; a son! A few months later, I began to perceive a change. I couldn't believe it, but it was as if he were jealous of Lee and Wade and resentful of the demand they made on my time and attention. He would become petulant and withdrawn behind a stony wall of cold silence. We were constantly moving through this period; every six months he would find a "better" job and we would uproot ourselves again.

I had begun to have problems with depression since my mother's death. I felt like we had reached another crisis point in life. I was using religion to compensate for my coping difficulties. Through faith and prayer, I felt I could overcome these problems in my personal life. However, problems were becoming steadily worse. I was in a state of denial. I was using religion to keep from facing reality.

And the reality was rapidly taking on a more nightmarish quality. The "dark person" that was his other self was about to emerge never again to be controlled, and never again to leave. He began to treat me very badly. He became increasingly critical of me, very patronizing, and demeaning.

He began to launch verbal attacks on me for no reason. It would be over the most insignificant things. He one time snarled his contempt at me that he hated my laugh. He said that it was such a fake laugh that he "could not stand to hear it." If I was what he considered lax in jobs around the house, it would be a tirade in words such as, "What did you do all day? You don't work, you don't help with the money, why couldn't you at least have the house in order? That was all you had to do, why wasn't it done?" He also began to be critical of my family. He was developing an air of superiority over everyone.

He became more and more critical of me, more irritable, and more volatile. The smallest thing could set him off. My personal appearance was criticized, my friends were criticized, and my sexual performance was criticized. Although I was very hurt and bewildered by this behavior, I felt that he was reducing me and criticizing me to feel better about himself. I had two children in two years; they both were babies requiring lots of caring, and I was being raked over the coals. Whenever he came home, which wasn't often, he would criticize me.

This was the beginning of the end. The disease was here to stay after seven years of marriage. This disease has many masks and many disguises. In my husband's case, it disguised itself under his substance abuse. I now believe that the substance abuse exacerbated the underlying psychosis which was always there but had hid behind a lifestyle of drug abuse, and was later to be misdiagnosed as such. He was heavily into drug use at this time. The use of hallucinogens had stopped but the amphetamine addiction was full blown.

He was working midnights and working a lot of overtime. He had been immersing himself more and more with the partying crowds but had gravitated towards one particular male friend (Mark). They would meet after work to go out drinking and smoking pot. He would come home a lot of times so drunk, Mark was half carrying him. He came home just to go to bed, to get up, take some more speed and go back to work again. I was very angry at him and resentful of his friend. They were inseparable. I was very jealous of this person and intensely disliked him. It was much easier for me to blame his friend for his behavior than to accept what was really happening, and place the responsibility where it belonged. I was also beginning to suspect that my husband's attachment to this person had homosexual overtones.

Despite all these problems, our sexual relationship was not affected. He was not an openly affectionate or nurturing person; sexual expression was his vehicle for tenderness and caring. It was our misuse of sex that made us compatible; each of us attempted to fulfill emotional needs denied to us as children through sex and that led to its corruption.

I was trying to get my husband to go for marriage counseling. Our lives were joined in the blood of our children. I was beginning to feel desperate about the outcome of my life. I started using tranquilizers, legitimately prescribed, to try to cope with everything that was happening. The deterioration continued. One night when my husband and I were making love, he told me that he and Mark had group sex with the same woman a few days before. He was very elated about this and wanted to repeat the experience with me. Not only had he discussed this with Mark, he also assured him that he would talk me into it. I felt like I'd been thrown into ice water. I felt degraded, cheapened, belittled, and betrayed. I felt he considered me a possession, a thing, a piece of meat.

When I regained enough control to speak, I confronted him with my feelings. Why would he do such a thing or think that I would be a party to that? He told me it was because he loved us both, and that I should do it because I loved him. He said it would make him happy to give the two people he loved to each other. This made me even more resentful of his friend. I was very embarrassed and humiliated to face him. I am a very private person and I could not bear to be the object of a discussion of this type. I was so angry at him, yet I felt ashamed; I felt that I must have done something to warrant this. But where could I go? I had no confidence in myself as a woman. I had little job skills. I had no support group. I had two small children dependent on me. There were no shelters for women where I could go. I stayed there and played ostrich to the seriousness of my situation.

He came home late one night. I was waiting up for him. As usual, I had no idea where he had been. When he came in he had the same cold and blank emptiness in his eyes that I had seen eight years before. He had blood all over his shirt. I was afraid. I didn't know whether he had been hurt or he had hurt someone. I felt a great unease with him as though he was a stranger, as though I didn't know what he was capable of. When I questioned him about it, he turned his gaze fully into my face and I saw the void in his eyes, an emptiness, and nothingness. I became truly frightened of him in that instant, and scared for him and my children. He was dazed. He did not know where the blood came from, and he had no recall of that incident, ever. I did not sleep that night. I had finally met that "darkness, blackness" he referred to eight years before.

He was quiet and withdrawn for a couple of days and when he ended his silence, it was to speak a death wish. He told me that he had hit a dog with the car on his way home. He had stopped to see about the animal, and as he watched his death throes, he felt envious. He said, "I wished it were me." Horrified, I asked him why he felt that way. He said, "Then I would be at peace." This was the first time he gave voice to a suicidal predisposition. It was longingly and wistfully spoken and came out of nowhere. I was horrified. I love life. Life is a great gift to be treasured. At its worst, it still holds hope. To hear a person long for death was an assault on life.

Mark was still very much a part of his life. Gradually, he became a part of my life too. At first, I was seething with animosity toward him, but with his irrepressible good humor and intelligence, he began to reach me. Despite myself, I began to like him and see the kindness of his nature. He penetrated my grief. I began to understand why my husband was so drawn to him. I started getting back in the social life with him and his wife. I felt like there might be hope for my marriage and my future.

But this was not to be. My husband was becoming more verbally abusive to me. He criticized everything about me. He told me I wasn't desirable. I was too fat. I lost all pride in myself. I really didn't have any idea what was happening. I needed my mother. I talked to my father. I let him see just enough to know that I was in one hell of a mess. I told him my suspicions of homosexuality. I told him about the drug abuse and of the economic hardship. He did not say, "Come home." He said, "Your mother hoped that you would never have children from that man." I don't think he even heard me. He had never heard me before. I don't know what made me think that it would be different now.

So, now what? "You've made your bed, now lie in it," was the clear but unspoken message. In my mind, I could hear him saying, "You made your choice, now you deal with it. He's your husband, take care of him, take care on your own."

He ended the conversation by saying, "He is demon possessed. I'll speak to him." Later, he gave my husband a good father-to-son chat about what a good woman I was, how much he should appreciate me, and love our children. My husband did nothing but agree. He did love me and the children. I was a good wife and a good mother. I went to church and prayed, and didn't he tell me he loved me so much, he'd never let me go? Yes, I was a "good wife." I was not forcing his hand and I was not making him face up to his personal responsibilities.

Though outwardly agreeing with my father, he was absolutely furious with me. I had broken his trust again. I had dared to criticize him and damage his confidence in me by talking about him to an outside person. I had exposed him to a person whose approval and respect he had wanted very badly. He was becoming extremely sensitive and touchy, so was his intolerance of criticism even when tactfully presented. His self-esteem was eroding. He was having serious problems with his sense of masculinity. He had such a rigid idea of what a man should be and he was failing himself and his standards of manhood. He believed that a man was emotionally strong and kept his problems to himself. A man was the "head of the house," responsible for all decisions, and whose word was law.

Austin lost his job and was unable to find another. I attempted to work at the time with two small children and the little work skills I had. I could only get minimum wage jobs. I had taken a job as a clerk in a convenience store which was run by a childhood friend of mine, a male. Although he was very open about his homosexual orientation, Austin was very jealous of him and made me miserable with his implications about my friend's true intent. He said that "faggot" was actually bisexual and he only wanted me there because he had a sexual interest in me. It was not possible for a man to have a woman for friend. This was an impossibility between a man and a woman. It was always generated by sexual attraction. With my good looks, I would generate lot of business for his store. I became more and more angry. I felt that he was misinterpreting everything about me.

This was a reflection of his attitude toward women in general. He would cultivate a "friendship" with attractive women, but it was sexually oriented, on his part. He was unable to relate to women in a personal way unless there was a sexual intent or attraction.

I didn't think that he was making an honest endeavor to find work. He told me, "I hate this town. This town has it in for me. I am black listed here. I will never be able to find work here or keep it." Later, he left again to find work with the promise that he'd be back again as soon as it was economically feasible.

During his absence, in an attempt to balm my own plummeting self esteem and alleviate my depression, I committed a sexual indiscretion with a man who had shown me kindness. Afterward, I felt very disappointed in myself. I felt hypocritical and dishonest. I intuitively felt it would be a grave mistake to confess this to my husband, and prayed that God would forgive me. With that, I felt it was settled; I had answered my own conscience.

A few months later, he came to take us with him. We started getting ready for the move. I called Mark, knowing that my husband would want to see him since we were moving away.

There was lot of comradery at the time of saying farewell between Mark and my husband. Mark, who had never touched me before, was a bit enthusiastic in good-byes to me. He gave me an affectionate parting kiss. At the time, my husband laughed; it was all part of the high spirit and good luck of the parting. But when he had me alone, he showed me his obsession with unfaithfulness. He began accusing me of having an affair with Mark in his absence. He was very steadfast and unshakeable in his belief. He would never see Mark or speak to him again. I was puzzled by his jealousy and anger since it was the same Mark with whom he wanted me to go to bed!

I would not bow before his wrath. I instinctively knew that it would be a horrible mistake. I was not prepared for the extent of the cross examination and the chipping away that he would resort to. Night after night, after the children were asleep, he relentlessly chipped away at me. He would brilliantly change his tactics from angry accusations to ultimate sorrow. At times, he would play on my guilt. He would give me a long speech, sometimes in parts, and sometimes the whole thing. It would run like this:

The real issue at stake here is your honesty. I have always felt that you were lacking in personal integrity. You were sleeping around when you were 16 years old. At least you were honest about yourself, then, because you loved me; you trusted me with the truth. You no longer love me. You no longer trust me to tell me the truth. This makes a mockery of this marriage. It makes a mockery of my manhood. If you felt that I were a real man you would trust me with the truth. I would forgive you, I always have. I love you with all my heart, but you **must** tell me the truth.

I never knew which tactic he would apply. He was a brilliant tactician and his mental cunning never showed as brilliantly as when he was attacking me. While all this went on, night after night, I still managed to hold a good paying job, and to get my toddlers into a decent day care.

He was venomous in his hatred and condemnation of Mark. Mark had extended a pure brotherly love to him, and to both of us, and I could not stand to see him maligned. One night I could stand it no longer. I told him about the extra-marital lapse I had in his absence. He went totally out of control. Before I knew it, he'd blacked my eye. My ears were ringing from his slapping of my face. He was choking me. I suppose I hit him to ward off this assault. He pinned my arms down and raped me repeatedly for the "slut" I was. He also sodomized me with violence. Interspersed with the physical assault was a litany of profanity. I was terrified, thinking that he was going to kill me. But the fact was that he did not want to kill me; he just wanted to humiliate me, inflict pain on me, and make me bear it. I had no defense against this ferocity.

When his rage and lust were spent, he went to sleep. I got up, took a shower, took my children to day care, and went to work.

The ravages of the night showed on my face. My eye was already discolored and swelling. The make up didn't hide the mottled color of my cheeks. I couldn't call in to take the day off because I had only had the job for two weeks. I did not want to lose the job. It was important that I find my own resources to get out of this situation. I felt I was all I had. So

I went in to work. Whereupon, I was promptly fired. A battered receptionist/switchboard operator was a visibly bad reflection for the company's image.

When I picked up the children and went home, he was at work. I was totally exhausted and emotionally numb. In our nine years of marriage, and in my entire life experience, nothing had prepared me for this. Yet, some inner strength warned me: It was just the beginning of physical abuse and sadistic sex and if I did not stop it, it would soon escalate. I knew that I could not allow this to happen.

So when he came at me again, I was mentally prepared for it. He got in a good hard first blow before I kicked him against the wall. I fought hard. And the whole time I was telling him, "You will not beat me again. I will not let you. I do not deserve this. I will fight you. I will fight you every time... You will have to kill me to keep me from fighting you. I will not tolerate this."

My initial reaction was of fear, rage, pain and a deep sense of violation. To be battered shreds and tatters your sense of security. I fought like my life depended on it; a life free of battering did, indeed, depend on it. He understood my message and retreated. He was a torn and fragmented person. He had a dark and bright side of him; a Jekyll and Hyde type personality.

When his bright side was up, Austin was the person that I had always loved. On the good side, he was a good father. He gave his full attention to Lee and Wade. He would bring them presents, read stories, and patiently teach them. He would rock them to sleep while stroking their hair, and singing lullabies. As a husband, he was helpful, considerate, and attentive. He was a hard worker, who celebrated life with his humor and generosity.

This person was thoughtful and kind. This person was generous and would give his last dollar to feed a hungry person. He would stand up for what he felt was right. He loved his children and would have fought to death to protect them. Then he could be manipulative and vicious. He could turn into someone I no longer knew.

There were indications that he was suffering from a disease. He was too preoccupied with my sexual past. He was too preoccupied with his suspicions of my unfaithfulness. There are warning signs of the illness, but you only see the good side of the person. Maybe my defensiveness was so strong, in the beginning, that I only saw in him what I wanted to see. It was the good person that I married and to whom I bore children.

I refute the charge of silent "masochist" that I still hear. I attempted to meet each problem head on. At no time did I just lie down and let him kick me. Neither did I just quietly let the madness overtake him. I fought his illness with every tool I had at my disposal because I loved him. I did not know what healthy love was. But I learned what it was not. Love is not a delusional and obsessive jealousy. He thought his jealousy was real love. My intellect had proceeded to try to seek answers and solutions to what was accruing. I would detach myself when things were calm at home, read psychology books, and try to make some sense of it all.

After my fighting back with him that night, his good side was back again. I was intuitive enough to realize that it wasn't over. Still shaken, I welcomed the reprieve.

Shortly after this, I was more traumatized, not by my husband but by another man. I was a victim of rape at knife point. I felt thoroughly defiled and so unclean. I cringed from my husband's touch. He used violence to make me tell him why I didn't want him to touch me, wrenching my arm behind my back. When I screamed in pain that I had been raped, he disbelieved me. He suspected that I had behaved provocatively and provoked this attack. Assuming the role of an interrogator, he had me go over it again and again until he was satisfied that there was no discrepancy in my story.

He felt that I should prosecute. I refused to do it. I felt that I would be on trial and I would be asked to prove that the rape did in fact occur. I could not go through that experience. I had expended my strength. He interpreted this as an evidence of my guilt. I would not be vindicated by a court of law.

The fight had been knocked from me. Bruised and in great deal of psychic pain, I limped to the security of my father's home. In defense of my father, I **never** bluntly told him the realities of my marriage. His own emotional make-up and my defenses created a gulf between us that could not be bridged. The whole time I was there, I kept wondering if I could build the bridge and enable him to be a parent to me and see me as an individual with my own life, needs, and dreams. But that was never to be. The unspoken message always was, "Fulfill your own responsibilities." He loved me on his own terms, with all his capabilities, but we could not reach each other. The night, before I was to leave his home, was spent in tearful sleeplessness.

What an awesome and terrible thing to literally believe the phrase, "for better or worse." Everything in my upbringing had conditioned me to believe this was an ultimate truth. You did not desert your brothers, sisters, husbands, or wives, if they developed schizophrenia, manic depressive illness, or any other handicapping illness. It came with the territory when you committed to the marriage. My religious training had made me believe that we were joined in the eyes of God. What God has joined, let no man or woman put asunder. After all, you were your brother's keeper and you would want them to do unto you if you were the one that was laying in the ditch. Self-sacrifice, that's what was called for. Strength, that's what was called for.

Yet, I began to feel that I was serving the needs of the religion rather than my own. I was tired of passively laying my burdens on Him and waiting for a miracle. I finally seized my life in my own two fragile hands and vowed that I would seek a resolution and not wait for the miracles to happen. I ceased to be a passive and dependent person.

I returned to him once again and was pregnant for the third time. I discovered that the monster of jealousy is one of manipulation, control, and immeasurable fear. This fear is a mutual fear. The jealous partner is crippled by his fear of losing the other partner. This gives birth to an irrepressible rage. As the disease becomes more firmly entrenched, the victim-partner becomes afraid for her life. My husband had found out that battering had not been an effective weapon, so his fear was growing. Although, I had met his violence with a rage of my own, my fear was still growing. My resolve was to defend myself. I would not assault, not instigate, but I would certainly defend myself.

After my return, there was a short period of calm. Recovering from the assault on my mind that the marital rapes had unleashed, I prayed that the darkness would recede for ever. How I prayed that the good side of his would prevail.

In spite of all that had happened, Austin was my husband and I loved him. When he would make love to me, I began to be responsive. This would also be used as a weapon against me. My desire for him prompted him to accuse me of being "insatiable" and "oversexed." The next episode that occurred foreboded the coming storm. He became morosely quiet and spent his time at home, in bed, sometime sleeping or just lying. He didn't bathe and didn't sleep well in the night. If I woke up in the night, I would find him staring at the ceiling. He only picked at the food I carried in to him. I could see the darkness of the storm gathering in his eyes. He would look at me coldly as though I were something inhuman. He would not touch me. I would go to sleep to the sounds of his masturbation. Violence seemed to be gathering within him, and the oppressive silence was thick with tension. My unease grew. I became fearful that he would become violent again. I told the children that Daddy was not feeling well, and they mustn't disturb him. I tried to entertain them and keep them occupied.

This period of "blackness" lasted three days. He broke his withdrawal by turning to me with sexual overtures. I responded to his kisses and embraces. I felt it was essential that I show my love for him. If he needed physical reassurance of this love, then I felt I should give him that. When he succeeded in his seduction, he began his sexual tirade against me. He told me that I was never raped and if I was I brought it on myself. It was in the way I looked and the way I moved. Every man could read me. I gave out the "come on" to every man because I was insatiable. Hadn't I just proved it by allowing him sexual access after he hadn't bothered to speak to me for three days?

He adamantly insisted that I had been sexually involved with Mark. I was a "slut" that had taken his best friend from him. One time, while making love, he whispered, "Was Mark that good?" instead of the appropriate words of love and caring. I froze instantly. This was countered with "You were never frigid with him. You couldn't get enough of him, could you?" The physical assault had changed into a mental and emotional assault.

I would cry and ask him how he could say these things to me. Once he broke down and tearfully told me it was because he loved me so much more than life itself. It was because I'd hurt him so badly; this treatment was in "direct proportion" to the pain that I had caused him. That, he'd loved me and I'd betrayed him with my infidelities. He said, "I love you so much Holly, you've done this to me." Such pathos. Such inconsolable grief. I wept for him. I pleaded for acceptance. I denied the wrongful accusations. I begged him to understand.

But there was to be no understanding, empathy, compassion or forgiveness for me. I think he was incapable of these qualities. I tried to communicate with him. Whatever I said, he twisted it into something else. If I cried, broken hearted, in his twisted way, he took that as an affirmation of love. When the storm was past, it was as though it had never happened. There was no remorse, or even acknowledgment that it had occurred. That was the most incredible part. He would never say, "I am sorry." It was very disorienting and bizarre.

That was the cycle. It was to increase in frequency and intensity because I was pregnant. He would never fully acknowledge this child. I found myself in an extraordinary position. I just could not believe that he was doing these things. If I allowed myself to think about it, I attempted to tell myself, "This is the last time it will ever happen. Surely he knows how much I love him." I looked for answers. I would carry the young children by my side and haunt the local library. I voraciously read every book--seemingly related--that I could get my hands on. The only things that seemed to have some insights were the theories of "sociopathic personality" and the "misogynist" men but there was no apt name for this horror I was living with. The answers weren't there.

I grasped at straws. I desperately wanted to believe that he could change and one day it would be over. At times, I felt I was responsible, that my behavior somehow had contributed to this. At times, I thought if I change some more, I can thereby effect a change in my partner. But, **never** did I feel that I needed this hell or that I deserved this treatment. Nor was I dependent on this person's madness and obsession to feel needed and loved. I was no longer dependent on him for my emotional needs. I was realizing that he was totally incapable of a loving relationship because he had no love for himself. He had no respect for himself, or he would not have felt the constant need to validate his existence and worth through sexual expression. Sexual expression was his validation of being a man and of being loved. This is what had led to its perversion and corruption.

Yet, it was during this time that he adopted an old man. He would take him to town to shop for his groceries and conduct his business. He would go by and check on him, and see to his physical comfort. He was capable of such contradictory behavior.

I have forgotten much of those nightmarish times, but there are things that stand out with remarkable clarity. One such memory concerns a particularly bad episode. His viciousness was incredible. Everything that I had ever done or he had ever **imagined** I'd done, was thrown in my face. I'd cried all night and he still wouldn't stop; the accusations, the sexual slurs, the name calling, the sexual battery, I was exhausted from attempting to defend myself. He continued his verbal abuse as he was getting ready for work. He was car pooling in those days, and he walked out to meet his fellow riders as a totally different man; chameleon like, laughing, joking, an instantaneous change into the good ole boy. I can still hear him laughing and talking to them that morning. It was my first time to see how the monster in him changed so fast for sake of the outsiders; but it was not the last time.

The second unforgettable memory is of his being in bed, and very withdrawn. Until this point, the disease had not impaired his ability or willingness to work. He was still striving to maintain the role of a good provider. That morning, I brought him coffee and breakfast and asked him about going to work. He looked at me and said, "You slut, you're not worth going to work for." He did not go to work for a week. I was bewildered. How could so much hatred and so much so-called love exist together? What madness was I dealing with?

He also began to accuse me of having a sexual interest in his new close friend. This was bizarre since this friend of his and I openly despised each other and on occasions had heated arguments. I would avoid him on purpose and hardly ever came into contact with him. He also accused me of blatant sexual interest with a co-worker of his with whom I had only exchanged a few words.

He would watch me constantly and his suspiciousness of me was growing steadily worse. He was also sexually coercing me. If I, for any reason, said no to a sexual overture of his, he would go into an immediate cycle of withdrawals, rage, and recriminations. My defense was to be one of passive resistance. I cannot describe the face of a horror, made all the more terrible because it was directed at me. I was looking at the fragmentation of a person I loved; a person being ripped apart by a relentless, hideous, crippling insanity. He was still capable of great kindness, yet, immeasurable rage. I truly believed that family was the foundation, marriage bond binds you in sickness and in health, and love abideth all things. What a terrible thing it is to believe that you are bound into such a relationship! I felt that he could not recriminate me if I did not give him even the remotest cause, so I isolated myself from outside contacts. I quit wearing make-up and stayed home as much as possible. But that did not help.

I spoke to my physician about his behavior. I did not mention the abusive behavior and the sexual jealousy. I only told him about his not talking to me and the time he spent in the bed. My physician told me that he thought my husband was depressed over the pregnancy. He said it was known to happen, though rarely, and I shouldn't be overly concerned. I unquestioningly accepted this and hoped he was right.

In my seventh month of pregnancy, I started bleeding. I was ordered bed rest as much as possible. My husband also let me rest. I had a difficult delivery, another son. He was a beautiful baby, a male version of his sister. But something was different. There was no fatherly pride in the child. There was no exuberance and no celebration. He told me, "He's your baby, you name him." At the time, I didn't grasp the significance of this statement. My children had not been yet been used as a weapon against me.

A friend of mine had taken my older children for the day to let me rest. My baby was sleeping. I was resting when he came into the room. He lay down with me and put his arms around me. Then he told me in the most degrading, gutter sex language, "I am going to have sex with you. I am going to do this because I know you are going to leave me. You are going back to the other men and I am going to stretch you and rip you. You will never be good in bed again." Then he held my arms down and did what he said he was going to do. I begged him not to do this, it hurt me. But it was useless. Our son was only ten days old, then!

I did not go back for my postpartum examination. I did not want to know the extent of the damage. I have since been told that there are tears in the vaginal wall and I need a hysterectomy to repair the damage. All of this in the name of "love." All of this because of "what you have done to me."

I did not yet know to what depths of despair this battle would take us. I knew that I had already paid enough in pain and blood. I would never have believed that he was capable of the behavior he exhibited toward me in the past year and a half.

I broke. I could not stand it anymore. I vowed to myself to leave him even if I had to crawl to my father's house. When the baby was four months old, old enough to travel, I made a 36-hour ride by bus. I had my three children, the clothes on my back, my suitcases, twenty dollars and a determination to begin a new life.

I did not tell anyone what I had endured. I was very much aware of the bias and bigotry with which the society dismisses women like me. "She must like it," is a slur I have heard over and over again. A destructive relationship places a woman in a very vulnerable position. She is embarrassed, emotionally isolated, and dependent for financial support. She is living a nightmare, too afraid to wake up or run. The man makes a concentrated effort to keep her dependent, disoriented, and dominated.

After our relocation, I soon obtained work. It was little better than minimum wages but I could manage. I paid my father a weekly rent, I bought my share of groceries, paid the sitter, and tried to be a responsible adult. There wasn't enough money to save towards financial independence, but when I could, I would put a little back for the dream of my own home, transportation, and independence. Although I still had a great deal of difficulty being able to relate to my father, I was grateful for the refuge and once again attempted to be the "good" daughter. I would take the babies alongside me and help my father with the work on the farm. I also managed his household.

I lived for my children. I was determined to be strong for them, to work for them, and one day make a home for them. I would sit up at night with them in their illness and go to work in the morning. Yet they weren't happy. They were having difficulty adjusting to a working mother. And they missed their father terribly. He had been wonderful to them. They missed his taking them places, bringing them presents, and playing with them. In their childlike world, they had lost their father and their mother.

Their father kept calling. He would call at first to talk to the children. How could I deny them this? He sensed his advantage and he was learning fast to use it. He worked on this. He began to talk to me and would tell me how much he missed having his family and that he still loved me. He said he wanted to change. I still wanted to believe that he could. I urged him to get help. I told him that I still loved the good side of him and I hated to see the dark side win.

While at my father's home, Mark and his wife became my support people. They opened their home to me. Laughter and friends once again entered my life. Yet, I felt different somehow; a sense of shame. Mark and I talked for hours about my husband. We had both loved him and we had both lost him to this disease. We talked about the possibility of involuntary commitment for my husband for hospitalized treatment, but I felt that it would be a dangerous thing to do. Having borne the violence at his hands, I did not dare underestimate his ability for violence. I knew how vindictive and volatile he could be. I felt that if I were to violate the veneer of normalcy that he presented to the world, there would be retribution. Undoubtedly, he could be a dangerous man and Mark agreed.

I did not tell Mark or his wife the extent of the abuse. Yet, I think Mark sensed this and he helped me hold myself up and helped me to heal.

Mark died in an accident. They said he died an instantaneous death. I was devastated. My entire support system was gone. Yet, my desolation paled in comparison to my husband's reaction. He called me on the phone. He had a gun in the room. He was clicking the chamber and saying he was going to "blow my brains out." For two hours, I used every resource I had to see him through his crisis. But I was 1400 miles away from him.

I contacted his mother. It had been his position that his mother had never loved him. As a mother, that was inconceivable to me. I felt she had to help him as she was all he had. I minced no words. I told her exactly what had occurred, and my feeling that she should have him committed. She reassured me that she would go to him that morning. Yet, he said, she never even called him. Nor did she call me.

I went to my local mental health clinic. I was given the latest information available on suicide and was advised that he was not my responsibility. The psychologist told me that he was a "sociopath" and I would never have any peace as long as he was part of my life. I had done all that I could do.

Yet, his pain had touched a chord within me. He was suffering and he was alone in this. Inwardly, I felt that I had forsaken him to this illness that he could not help and could not control. We talked a lot on the phone during this time. He had been frightened by the intensity of his emotion and by the fact that a week of his life had passed of which he had no memory. He assured me that he would seek psychiatric help. I was relieved.

A couple of weeks later, my father told me that I would have to find another place to live. He was selling the farm and he could not help me anymore.

After 18 months of struggling, scrimping, and striving to become independent, I had very little. Not enough to establish myself, buy a car, or make a home for my family. I could see no solution. I had tried and failed. I felt like I had failed in everything. I felt a failure as a mother. I had such sad little children. I had failed to provide a home for them.

The next time my husband called promising to get psychiatric help, promising to give up the drugs, telling me how much he loved the children and me, I told him that I would return. My intuition was screaming, "Don't do this!" but I denied my intuition and my judgement. I denied the horror that I had experienced earlier. My maternal side was saying, "You can bear this for the sake of your children." My conscience was screaming, "Do not desert him to this!" I wanted to save him by sheer force of will. I was still young enough and hopeful enough to believe that it was possible. I was still in mourning. I was forlorn.

I thought if his mother would not fight for him, then I would. I would not desert him, nor forsake him. I had in effect assumed full responsibility for him. I had become his caretaker. I did this with the expectation that he would keep his word. I did not yet know the progressive and degenerative aspect of this disease.

Again, there was a short period of peace. He was elated to have his family with him again. When he was secure in our unification, he refused to go to a psychiatrist. He had obtained his desire, there was no need to keep his word. Denial was his defense. He was so lacking in self-esteem that he could never admit to having a mental disability.

To begin with, there was an exclusive time when we celebrated life as a family. He was still capable of being a good father. Yet, there would be times when he would look at the youngest child with an odd and puzzled expression. He was very critical of my relationship with our youngest child. He would tell me that I was spoiling him. He would ask, "Who is he [Craig] named for?" Also, there was a marked lack of the doting attentiveness he had displayed earlier toward the other children.

He revealed the reason for this during one of the cycles. He broke his silence with the question, " Who is Craig's father?" There was so much resemblance between him and this child which proclaimed to the rest of the world who the father was; yet, the distortion of this disease prevented him from seeing what was glaringly apparent.

The cycles again were prevailing within our intimate relationship. In these cycles, he would question me about my sexual activity behind his back. I would answer him clearly and matter-of-factly, but without elaboration.

On one occasion, I asked him the following:

If I am such a bad person, why do you still want me? I don't understand this. It should be obvious to you that I am totally wrong for you. Why don't you just try to find someone who could give you the love you need?

He gave me this answer:

There could never be another woman. I have nothing to commend me to this world. I am not successful or educated, but I have you. You are the most beautiful, intelligent, and kind person that I have ever known. People look at you and they know that I am special because you are mine.

He used sex aggressively. He would sexually coerce me. I developed a defense to the sexual coercion by separating my emotions from what my body was experiencing. I had become adept at staring at the ceiling waiting for it to be over. He was alone in that place.

He began to rely heavily on fantasy during this time. There was predominantly a voyeuristic theme to these fantasies. He would fantasize watching me engage in sex with another man without the rival male's knowledge of his presence. In this fantasy, he would see himself in a closet or another room while masturbating. At times, I felt he might attempt to make this fantasy a reality. I once came home to discover that he had drilled a hole in the wall from the bathroom to our bedroom.

He also repeatedly attempted to persuade me to engage in group sex, with him and another male partner. This would follow a pattern that he had established in his previous encounter with group sex. In those encounters, foreplay would be enacted by both partners. Then the rival would have intercourse first, while he watched it masturbating. Then he would follow the rival with penetration. He would say, "You should have made love to Mark. He would have loved it." I found this to be disgusting.

Strangely, a fantasy was not a threat to him. However, in reality, if he saw another man looking at me when we were in public, he would become furious. If someone on the sidewalk or passing in the car looked at me, he would make an obscene gesture, or if we were in a restaurant and a man would look at me casually, he would look at him in a challenging way, as if saying, "I know what you are doing. Come on, dare."

The violence toward me was at its lowest ebb during this time; possibly, because he had bolstered his self-esteem through sexual interaction with other women during our separation. His anger was being directed toward the world. He would use the automobile aggressively and dangerously. For example, if he were being followed too closely, he would slam on his brakes. If a person made a driving error, he would force them off the road before he would give. On one occasion, while I was with him, he became enraged at me and began to drive dangerously. He was driving so fast I didn't think I would get out alive. He told me, "I don't care if I die, I'll take you with me." He would frequently have fights at work with other men. He was using marijuana heavily and would occasionally miss work. He was very vindictive. At one time, he took on three men in a fight and emerged unscathed.

During this period, the cycles were dominated by his grief. He mourned his friend, and with pathos and recrimination attempted to instill guilt in me. He would start talking about Mark and start crying. If I attempted to comfort him, he would become furious. He told me, "It's your fault that I lost my brother. I loved him and you took that away from me. You couldn't leave him alone. He is gone and I was angry with him! He died without knowing I loved him, because of you. Get away from me." I too was in pain from his death. I refused to bear Austin's responsibility and guilt. My pain would not allow Mark to be the object of contention. At times, I would use silence as a defense. At other times, I would say, "You made those decisions. You shut him out of your life. Your guilt is your own." I refused to allow Austin's continuing obsession with him. I would tell him, "Mark is dead. Don't do this."

I had strengthened myself against these multi-faceted attacks by telling myself that his perception of me did not make it *truth*. It was only his perception of my reality, and not my reality. He knew nothing of the inner person in me. He could not be my conscience. I rejected his perception of me and was able to forgive myself and answer to myself.

This enabled me to become more assertive about what had occurred in the past and the woman that I had become. The darkness of his disease was losing power over me. Yet my fear was increasing. With each cycle, I wondered what new horror would emerge. Once he came up on me in my sleep and clamped his hand around my ankle. It frightened me so badly, I jerked away and kicked him in the chest and he was flung away from me. I told him I had been having a nightmare, but I was amazed at the primal fear that incident revealed.

At the same time, I was becoming more aware of the factors in his life that contributed to his problem. The primary factor was the void of his self-esteem. I felt that needed to be addressed. I attempted to do this through positive affirmation and by discussion of the problem when he was approachable. I would attempt to encourage him to summon the strength to fight these "bad moods" as he called them. I would tell him, "You do not have to give in to this. Push it away from you. Do not allow yourself to think this way. It's harmful to us. It's hurtful to you. Be strong." He would sorrowfully say, "I can't. I can't," or angrily say, "You do not know how strong I've already had to be!"

My growing awareness enabled me to separate the disease process from the man. In that way, I would remain able to relate to the man.

He was very suspicious of my motivation for coming back. He would ask me, "Why did you come back?" He never felt assured that love was the motivation for this. As far as he was concerned I never loved him, ever. He would tell me that I didn't know what love was. No matter what I did, it was never enough. He knew that my relationship was not good with my father, he suspected that since it did not work out with my father, that was the real reason I came back to him.

One time he told me "Why did you bother me by coming back? I was having an affair with a 19-year old woman." In reality, there was nothing like that. The reality was his calling and calling on the telephone to talk to me and the children. The way he talked then, you would not have thought there was anybody there for him.

During this time he would say, "This was a good experience for you getting away from me because you found out that nobody else would ever really want you but me. You found out that children were a liability. Men just want to be with you and have sex with you, but as far as any commitment, no body would do that but me. No body would ever love you as much as I do."

At times, he would talk about committing suicide. This was not in terms of what had previously occurred; but in connection to his feelings for me, "I would kill myself if you ever left me again." Later, these suicidal talks became part of the cycle.

Once this disease of jealousy sets in, it goes in only one direction, it progresses. Once the mood cycles, recriminations, and sexual accusations begin, those are always there. The suspiciousness, negativity, and paranoia grow. There is no improvement, only deterioration. At times, there is a greater threat of physical violence than other times. If you are hoping that it will go away on its own, this will not happen! Once this behavior is entrenched, it continues and intensifies. There is not enough reassurance, there is not enough comfort for this person, there is not enough of anything within you to change this behavior. There is no remission here. Once it begins, it progresses relentlessly. Every area of the affected person's life becomes contaminated.

It was growing worse, as his anger with me continued to grow. As the disease progressed, there was an overall deterioration of his personality. He was increasingly withdrawing from everyone which affected his relationship with children, too. As his anger grew with me, so did his inability to parent his children. The least provocation could cause an angry outburst. The cycles began to be less clearly defined.

I tried to compensate for his behavior with our children, more so with the youngest child. He was critical of my relationship with Craig. Of all children, Craig was specially targeted. He would look at him and say, "You are spoiling him." At the same time, he was partial and showing favoritism towards Wade. This intensified and complicated sibling rivalry. The injustice of Austin's behavior began to alienate Lee from her father. With the passage of time, each of the children would come to a greater realization of the partiality expressed by Austin and they began to balance it in their own way.

He had certain expectations from the children which at times were beyond their developmental level. If I felt he was expecting too much from any one of them I would intercede. His expectations and his attitude were dependent upon what mood he was in and where he was with his thought processes. At times, I felt if I could make him see that he was being too stringent, our lives could be happier. He became increasingly domineering toward me and the children. They were also becoming the object of his misdirected anger, sarcasm, overreaction, and derision. His method of disciplining was inappropriate and extreme. The least provocation could trigger this behavior. This was intolerable to me. He felt he had to be the authority over me, the children, and my relationship with the children. He would do this through belligerence, belittling, and reducing behavior.

When I would intervene to save the children from his behavior, it would escalate to physical fighting. One such incident happened when I was correcting them and he overheard it from the next room. He came in to the kitchen and began a tirade against us. He told me, "You don't know how to correct these boys. They don't listen to you." He mimicked me in a falsetto voice saying, "Boys, stop please!" Then he turned on them with anger, "You don't respect your mother. You will respect your mother." I was very angry at him for undermining my authority. I asked him, "Please leave me and let me handle this! He refused and then he continued to discipline them. I told him, "You get out of here and allow me to be a mother to these children. You do not have the right to override my authority. You are reducing me in their eyes." He still continued with them, ignoring my request. I became very angry and pushed him on the chest screaming, "You get out. Get out of here! You have no right to reduce me in front of my children. Let me be their mother!"

My anger was superseded by my concern. I felt I was losing my ability to protect the children from Austin's volatility and they were losing confidence in my ability to protect them from his anger.

His relationship with his family and my family also became affected. Once his sister-in-law planned Christmas dinner. It was to be a family reunion of sorts. Austin refused to go. He told me, "It is a farce. They don't love me. I'm not going." He was also very reticent around my family at the family gatherings. He was growing very paranoid. He wasn't comfortable with either of our families. He felt he was the focus of our attention. He would ask me, "What were you talking to your sister about, were you talking about me? I saw you look over at me. What were you saying?"

He was also jealous of my family. He didn't like for me to go anywhere with my sisters, to go to their house, to go out for lunch or to go shopping. He tried to be very limiting in what he would allow me to do. If I proceeded to do those things, he would be very angry. But I was no longer willing to isolate myself; I wanted to have a regular life. It would threaten him that I chose to be with other people. It was like he wanted me to be his, just his.

It would be worrisome for me if I wanted to do something different. Sometimes, I would attempt to cushion myself by taking the children with me. I thought he would know that if I had taken the children with me, there would be nothing that I could do with three children around me. However, it would make no difference. The accusations were continuous regardless of my behavior.

As the disease progressed, all men that he came in contact with were suspect. Although he was still outwardly functional, his internal suspiciousness, paranoia, and watchfulness was growing. He felt that everyone was a "con" and out only for what they could use you for. He became unable in the later part of his life to build lasting relationships. He would inevitably assume that they were only being friends with him to get to me.

My reaction to this was to retreat from any social contact with his acquaintances. If it was possible for me to avoid them, I did. In that way, I made concessions to his convoluted thinking.

When it was still a secret battle, one night, Lee overheard one of his raging, crying tirades. She began to isolate herself, and from that point onwards, really shut him out of her life. She was very upset over this and questioned me. I had always been very honest with my children, so I attempted to make her understand what she had overheard. She was shocked and couldn't believe that he was saying these things and making me cry. She said, "I hate him." I tried to make her understand that he was sick but it was too much for her to comprehend and come to terms with.

I could see further deterioration when the accusations that had been, at an earlier time, discussed only in the privacy of the bedroom, began to be discussed in front of the children. It disturbed me even more that he would make these accusations and allusions in front of the children; I perceived these to be mindless assaults on my integrity. We had huge fights about it because he had already browbeaten me for years about these things. Now it was to further damage my relationship with my children. I was also concerned that it would damage their perception of male-female relationships. Even if he saw me talking to another man, this was grounds for suspicion and accusation. I would refute his accusation, at times angrily and loudly, other times, quietly by saying, "You know that it's not true. I refuse to discuss this with you."

I had finally become strong enough to put it in proper perspective. It had nothing to do with me, it was him. I became much more assertive in our interaction. That infuriated him. That's when the suicidal discussions became the ultimate weapon. These discussions were not vague statements anymore, but were graphically described. He would always make me cry with his suicidal discussions. When he would make me cry, that was affirmation of love. This enabled him to regain the emotional advantage and reestablish power and control. I felt that on one hand, it was manipulation and coercion on his part, and on the other, his anger and desperation was growing. He was becoming more dangerous and assaultive and when I would fight back, his suicidal discussions would intensify. I knew that he was capable of committing suicide and also taking me with him. I wanted to protect the children from that, so I had to withdraw from his anger, pain, and desperation.

At times, my withdrawal would reduce him to tears; then he would talk about committing suicide and say, "I don't want to do this but you are making me do this because you don't love me and I can't live without your love." He was making me responsible for his very life!

Because I realized that suicide was a very real possibility, my attempt to deal with these issues became more urgent. I was very straightforward in my attempt to make him see that he was diseased. I addressed this and in all of its ramifications. Yet, he would not attempt to change his thoughts; he basically fed his own illness with such thoughts. He would start by watching me. This would give him some ideas and he would focus on them until they became real to him. He would take one innocent remark or gesture and build upon it. This was what had developed with his jealousy, feelings of worthlessness, and with his inability to accept my love for him. He had fed these feelings and made them real for himself.

Lending himself to jealousy, he focussed on my sister's husband, David, for six years before his death. He dwelt on it. He would accuse me of sexual intent and misconduct. Although such accusations were baseless, they would become more and more real to him. My relationship with David was built on familial love, mutual respect and friendship that he and I had developed through the years. I always denied this allegation and he never had any reason to suspect more was involved, yet his suspicion of David, grew to dangerous proportions.

Another erosion which showed the progression of his disease was in our sexual relations. He became incapable of sexual intercourse with me unless I was asleep. His self-esteem was so eroded and his feelings of inferiority so intense, he felt that he was not a man anymore. He would initiate sex, then he would look at me and say, "I know you don't want me. You don't love me." Then he would withdraw over to his side of the bed and just lay there, so desperate!

I also attempted to deal with his increasing dependency on me. This dependency was that of a child on his mother. In every area of his life, he was dependent on me. I was earning the living, I was physically and emotionally caring for the family, and I was caring for him. He was physically very dependent on me by this point. If I didn't cook for him, he wouldn't eat. I would have to prod him, "Go, I think you need to take a bath." He then expected me to come and scrub his back. I would tell him, "I am not your mother." But that was what it had become.

I was angry because he was so dependent, yet so punishing. He was so sad and pathetic, yet so assaultive and vicious. One morning, he was trying to wake me up and I wouldn't. He took his foot and planted it squarely in my lower back and literally kicked me out of bed saying, "WAKE UP SLUT!" I was running out of strength. I didn't think it could get any worse, but it was worsening. His anger and animosity were growing. Craig and I were targeted. I had to do something to try stop it.

In attempting to stop it, I would tell him, "I can't be responsible for you. You have to be responsible for yourself and get help for yourself. You have things that you have to answer for, the way you treat these children. Lee has a hard time dealing with the way you treat Craig. It's totally unfair. I've been telling you for the last three years that you've been turning the children against you because of the way you act.

You are a man.   You have a responsibility to us and to yourself."

His disease was no more a personal illness of his, it had become a disease of the family, severely affecting each one of us. He was unable to comprehend that it would affect us. He could say and do terrible things to me and the children and expect that it should not interfere with anything. His defensiveness was tremendous; he could still totally deny all these things.

One night, Austin, Wade, Craig, and I had gone out. Austin was very hostile towards Craig that night. Craig was very nervous around Austin because he realized that whatever he would say, Austin would jump on him. So Craig was not saying anything. Austin was asking us what did we want to do and where did we want to go. He was becoming angry because we were unable to reach a decision. None of us wanted to do the same thing. This really irritated him. The boys started bickering over their ideas. Finally Austin decided we would go eat. Then he was scolding Craig for fighting with Wade. Craig was feeling dejected and upset. As we came to the restaurant, Austin told him to get out of the car. Craig didn't move fast enough. Austin grabbed him by his arms and jerked him out of the car. When he did this, Craig's head hit the top of the car, against the metal. He was crying and went to the restroom because he was so embarrassed. He couldn't eat in the restaurant and the meal was spent in total silence. It was disastrous.

I was furious with him and told him, "You are abusive to this child. You can't treat him this way." I was still angry when we got back home. I gathered up the children and told him we were going out for a while. I was thinking, "Where can I go?" I called him and told him that we were not coming home that night. I said, "I am not going to live in this hell anymore. These children are not going to live in this anymore." He said, "What did I do?" I said, "You think about it; but you find somewhere to go before I get home tomorrow. I'll be back tomorrow and I don't want you to be there."

We spent the night at my sister's house, sleeping on her sofas and floor. The next day, I was afraid to go home. I was afraid I'd find him dead in the house. When I returned home he was very much alive. He was telling me that he wouldn't leave. It was his home and his family and I had no right to kick him out. He further said he wouldn't live without me. I said, "These kids have been through enough. What you need to do is to go to a mental hospital and commit yourself. Get the care that you have been telling me for years that you would. It is not just you and I anymore. You are hurting these children and it has gone on too long and I can't tolerate it anymore." He angrily said, "You are full of shit."

Remaining calm, I said, "These children are afraid of you. I am afraid of you. Your behavior frightens us." Upon hearing this he was shocked and angry. Since he loved and trusted Wade, he asked him if that was true. Though Wade feared his father's unstable and unpredictable behavior, he was brave to tell him that was true. Hearing this, Austin cried. He called the children and apologized to them. He promised them that he would change. The children couldn't look at him.

I had heard promises of change. I knew he sincerely wanted to but was unable. When we were alone again, I told him it was too late for these promises of change. When I said that it was too late, he began to tell me that he would kill himself. He was speaking with more determination and longing than he had ever done before. I got out of the house and called the mental health center's emergency number. I told the clinician on duty that we were fighting and he was seriously suicidal. She told me that he was not my responsibility. She asked me if he would voluntarily come to the hospital. I told her, "No way because I have already tried that." She said, she would take whatever steps were necessary. She said she would send a policeman to my home and get him evaluated. I said, "That won't work because this man can completely change. I have seen it. They won't see anything wrong with him." She then said, "Then, you have to realize that you are not responsible. He can go to a mental hospital, stay there for two months, come out the next day and end his life." I said, "I understand that but let's try what we can."

She told me to go back home and stay with him until the policeman came. So I did. The children went in to one room and locked the room from the inside. Austin was very morose and very determined to end his life. I was trying to dissuade him. When the policeman came, it was a very touchy situation because I hadn't told Austin. I knew that he wouldn't subject himself to that. So when someone came and knocked on the door, I said, "I had to do this. If you wouldn't help yourself, I **have** to do what I think is right to get help for you." He didn't even get out of the bed, he just laid there and the policeman came in to the bedroom to talk to him. He said to the policeman, "You have no business here. I am not breaking any laws. I am not violent. I am not harming this woman. She wants to end this relationship. I am upset over that because we have been together for a long time. You can understand that, can't you?" He was very calm, coherent, and very much together. The policeman stayed there for a short time and when I went to see him out to the car, he said that he could see no justification to arrest him and take to the hospital. That's exactly what I had anticipated anyway. I had always been alone trying to deal with him. I was all there was. When I went back in, Austin proceeded with the discussion of suicide. The children didn't want to stay there. They were afraid but there wasn't anywhere to go.

Austin was furious. He told me, "I am going to take this gun, and I am going to drive out to the mountains, and I am going in to the woods, and I am going to kill myself. He was speaking calmly but he was so enraged. Crying with pain, anger, and frustration, I told him, "You just can't do this. You can't just go off and die like an animal." He told me, "I am waiting for the daylight. I don't want to die in the dark."

I knew he meant to do it this time. I kept trying to appeal to his love for us and his paternal side, the side of him that was "the good father." I kept saying, "I love you and your children love you. They need you. You are their father and they need your help." I told him he had a responsibility to them to fight this thing. He could not set an example of suicide for them. I said, "You can't make them go through that."

I continued to plead with him, "Austin! I love you but I can't stay in this with this fear we have of you and with this potential of harm. The children are terrified of you." In pleading with him, I was reduced to tears; but I firmly insisted that he must accept responsibility for his life and for **all** his children. He finally told me that he would go to get help. It was his last promise.

I called to get an appointment with the mental health clinic. He would ask me during this time, "If I go, will it be alright again?" I said, "You have to just go and see. You **have** to go and **try** to get better because you can't stay here and treat these children this way anymore. We have to just wait and see."

When I finally got him to go, he sat there very meek and quiet and said nothing. The therapist was looking at each of us trying to assess the problem. When directly questioned, he possibly answered three questions asked by the therapist. His attitude was one of bewilderment, effectively saying, "I don't know why I am here." At one point, he told the therapist, "I am here because she brought me. She says there is something wrong." When I realized there would be no real participation from him, I began telling the therapist about how angry he was, how we didn't get along with each other, and of the history of his substance abuse. I told the therapist about the cycles of rage, alternating with roughly three weeks of normal behavior and then two weeks of abnormal behavior. I felt that a chemical imbalance in his brain was causing these cyclical changes.

In the clinical interviews, I was in a terrible position. I was afraid that if I said something which could be twisted and blown out of proportion, I would pay for that. If I had a better understanding of the disease at the time, I could have made myself understood to the therapist; but I had not made the connection between his obsessive jealousy, his feelings of inadequacy, and his rage. However, even if I had made these connections, I could not have said those things in front of Austin.

I told the therapist of his suicidal intent. The therapist asked him about it and Austin explained, "I didn't want her to leave me." I told the therapist about my children's fear of him and he admitted, "My son told me that he is afraid of me, sometimes." He was very quiet, very submissive, allowing me to verbalize what the issues were. However, he did not address any of these issues himself, he just allowed me to do it. His passivity in the interviews conveyed his belief that the only help for him was up to me to give, no body else could.

Although I was unable to present the utter seriousness of the situation to the therapist, I managed to convey the fact of Austin's moodiness. The therapist attributed it to Austin's substance abuse which he denied. I had already ruled that out as the reason of his moods. Earlier, at my insistence, Austin had gone "straight" for a period of time. There had been no improvement; if anything, the symptoms worsened. Marijuana "high" became the closest he could come to normalcy in this last stage of the disease.

At my insistence, the therapist did set up an appointment for a psychiatric evaluation. His aversion to any kind of therapy reasserted itself on our way home. He said, "They have to blame everything on marijuana. I don't have a f---ing drug problem. I can quit any time I want to. This is about you. I couldn't talk to anyone about you. I couldn't tell them how much you've hurt me." He further told me, "You don't love me anymore. What could anybody say to me to change that?"

The day before his appointment with the psychiatrist, his defensiveness reemerged and he told me, "There is nothing wrong with me. This is your fault. I am not going. You call and break the appointment." I refused to do that. I was very angry at him but I controlled it because I had to get him to go for the sake of all of us. I was insistent that he go. He became more adamant in his refusal. I told him, "Don't even consider me in this, please go for the sake of the children."

This infuriated him. He told me, "You've turned these children against me. You've turned me in to the bad guy because you wouldn't discipline them properly. You made me more harsh than I would have been because you are not a good mother." I was very disappointed that he was so defensive and still resisting. It was a serious situation but I had done everything that I could do to get help. He did not keep the appointment. I knew it was the end. I had pursued every avenue I knew. It was six weeks before his death.

He, however, was trying to be more patient with children, trying to be more "normal" but it was something he couldn't control. When the symptoms started to reemerge, he was very quiet. He would quietly and with sorrow say, "You don't love me." It was absolute pathos, he still believed I did not love him. I told him that I had spent more time with him the past few months than I did with the children. I was asking him to fulfil his responsibility. Although, I wanted nothing more than for him to be well, my children had to be my priority. I still loved him, yet, I also hated him. My dream of "happily ever after" was sustaining me but I could no longer tolerate his mistreatment of us.

He felt that what I was really doing was pressuring him to make him leave. He started telling me, "You are only doing this because you want to be single. I think you want to be with David (my brother-in-law). You want a real man. I am not a real man to you. You want to be with other men." He became much more withdrawn because of these beliefs. He stayed angry and most of the time he wouldn't speak to me at all. When I attempted to talk about this behavior, he would become belligerent, "I'm not leaving. This is my home. If you try to make me leave, I will take you to court and take these children away from you. I'm not leaving."

He would sometime talk to Wade, that's all. He wouldn't eat anything that I cooked. If he wanted a sandwich or something, he would tell Wade to go and make it for him. If he had to ask me anything, he would tell Wade to ask me. He would scream out Wade's name and I would jump. He spent a lot of time in bed but he wasn't sleeping much. He also began to come home from work to see where I was.

Then, Craig got sick, really sick. When he kept getting worse I thought he had pneumonia. Since I was working and I already had taken a lot of time off, I asked Austin if he would take him to the doctor. He said he would but when I came home from work, I found out that he had not taken him to the doctor. That night I called my father and asked him to take Craig to the doctor. When my father came to take him, Austin refused to let him go. I came home from work and Austin was very nonchalant about this. I was furious. I started screaming at him, "You are abusing him. You are denying this child medical treatment and that's abuse. You have crossed the line and you can get out. You won't abuse the children again." I was furious and he knew it. I'd had it. I told him that I didn't care where he went and what he did but he didn't need to come around me anymore. He was very angry but he left contending that I was letting Craig manipulate me and that he just couldn't believe I was asking him to leave. He said, "I always knew Craig would come between us."

He left that afternoon. I arranged medical care for Craig, and I took him to sign up for ball at school. Austin came there and waylaid me. He said, "You can't make me leave. I don't have anywhere to go." I told him that he had his friends. He had his mother, brothers, and sister, and he could ask anyone of them to take him in for a while until he could make better arrangements. He told me that he couldn't ask them because they didn't love him or care about him. I said that he was a grown up man and I was sure he could handle his own problems. Hearing this, he went into another screaming tirade, "You don't love me. You never loved me. You don't care what happens to me." I told him that he could think whatever he wanted to but he wasn't going to live with my children and he wasn't going to be a part of my life anymore. So he left.

The next day, I went to consult the legal aid services to find out what I could do legally about this situation. I was told that legally he had a right to be in the house until I served divorce papers. I told them that he had been contending that he would not leave. I was told that the law said he didn't have to leave unless the landlord evicted him. I was glad Austin didn't know this. I initiated the divorce proceedings. When I came home, he was there in the house. He still had the house key which he was not willing to give to me. I came in and he acted as if he was still living there. I asked him, "What are you doing here?" He said, "Well you know, it is still my home." I said, "No it is not your home anymore and you are not welcome here."

At this point he became furious and menacing. His eyes were filled with hatred and rage. He started telling me, "You say this is about the children but what you really want is to be with other men. If you try to see anybody, I will kill him." Then he said, "I will do it where I can get away with it and no body will know that I did it but you will know. I will never leave you alone." I told him that he was a sick person and asked him how he could think that way. He told me that he knew that the real reason I was doing it was for David. I told him that I only felt respect for David for the way he took care of my sister in her illness. I said, "I like him and respect him as a person but I would never have an affair with him. I would never do that to my sister and I would never degrade myself by intruding in someone else's life. This is absurd."

He was pacing. His reply was, "You're a damned liar," and he started screaming a litany of profanity. I did not respond. Then, he quietly said, "I am going to kill him and I want to kill you. I might just kill you." He paused and looked directly in to my face. His features raged insanity. In his eyes, I saw pure rage and hatred. I saw DEATH; I felt my death was there in his eyes. Then he screamed, "I am going in to the bedroom right now and I am going to get the shotgun and I am gonna blow my f---ing head off. You want to come watch me?" He turned and started running towards the bedroom where the gun was. Terror washed over me. It was my ultimate fear. I ran outside. I could run no further than the car because my children were playing in the neighborhood. I was thinking, "He has always cared so much about what people thought about him, he won't follow me; he won't come out here and kill me in front of the neighbors, in broad daylight. He won't." I was listening to hear the gun go off. I could hardly breathe. He came out but he didn't have the gun. He told me, "You f---ing bitch! You are not worth it. But I am going to kill myself and I am going to kill David. You will be getting a call from the hospital." After this, he left.

Up to this point, I had not said anything to David about Austin. I didn't want to bring this problem to him. His father had died that very day. He was already overloaded, trying to deal with his grief. I knew my husband had never been so bizarre and I had never been so afraid. Arguing with myself and still capable of denial, I thought, "Maybe he won't do anything. Maybe this is the ultimate to try to get me to submit." I didn't know if it was his ultimate manipulation attempt, or if it was for real this time. I concluded it was manipulation since he had used fear and the threat of violence many times to coerce me.

He came in the next morning while I was asleep and let himself in to the house. It was about five o'clock on Saturday morning. He came in and woke me up by kissing me on the cheek. It scared me and I jumped up in the bed. My heart was pounding. He was very quiet. He said, "I haven't slept. Can we talk?" I got up. He was very calm. He said, "I don't know what I am going to do. I don't have anywhere to go. I don't have any family. I don't have my family anymore. There isn't anywhere for me to be." Still very calmly, he told me, "I really want to kill you, you know that. But I decided last night that I am not going to because these children need you. They need you too much and I love them too much."

Then he started talking about David and said, "I still want to kill David." I tried to appeal to his compassionate side because he had a compassionate side. I told him, "You can't do that. He has a young child. Her father is all that she has and you can't take that away from her. You can't be that cruel." To try to appease his mind, I told him, "I swear, as

God is my witness, there has never been anything between us, nor would there ever be. You **have** to believe me and you **have** to try to control these thoughts. Don't do this, it's wrong for you to do this Austin! This is not worth a human life." He still would not commit himself one way or the other. He would not say, "Alright, I won't." Then he left. It was very strange and terrible. He was so calm and yet the things he was saying were so insane and frightening. Even the calmness was frightening. How could he say that he was going to kill someone with such calmness?

When he left, I called the Women's Emergency shelter telling them what went on. The lady who took my call stayed on the phone with me for quite a while. However, she didn't grasp the seriousness of it. She kept on saying, "Well! My husband said this all the time; it's just manipulation, he won't do anything." I was very worried but I thought maybe she is right; I've heard him say that he is going to commit suicide but he hasn't. I wasn't very reassured. As I thought more about it, I said to myself, "Damn! He is coming in here on me in my sleep and saying these terrible things. Yesterday, I was running from him thinking that he was going to kill me. I had fought him for years, to the gates of hell and back, but I had **never** run from him. I had never felt that much fear of him. I had never felt that much fear, ever."

Compelled by these thoughts, I had to call the police and I told them exactly what was going on. They told me that he was still my husband and legally he could come in the house and say or do anything. They could only intercede if he became physically violent. They told me I could contact an attorney Monday who could arrange for a judge to grant me an injunction against him, an order of protection. Once an injunction was received, the police would enforce that; but that was all they could do. I told him that my husband was threatening another person's life. He asked me if he was carrying a gun. I said, "I don't know. He is not living with me anymore. He could get a gun and I wouldn't know it. He is not here." Again, the police told me under the law there was nothing they could do. He suggested I contact this person and tell him to guard his back. He said, "Call us, let us know if he gets a gun." I was again totally alone with this without any options or support.

The same day, while I was making lunch, Austin just walked back in. He was even more calm. I said, "Austin! What are you doing here?" He said, "Please! Let me come back." I said, "No! I can't. I can't watch you." I sat down and cried and I couldn't stop. He was stroking my hair, trying to comfort me. I couldn't stand it anymore and he wouldn't leave me alone. He said, "Holly, I can't stand to see you cry anymore." I told him, "Please! Just leave. Go away. Give me some peace. I can't stand anymore of this. I hurt for you. I've carried your pain. I can't carry it anymore. Go away and leave me alone!" I went in to the other room alone. He followed me. He started crying and said, "Would you please just hold me for a minute?" I said, "There is no point in this. I can't live with you. I can't give you shelter anymore." He said, "Please! Just hold me."

I put my arms around him and he put his head down on my shoulders. He was sobbing. He said, "Holly! you are my heart. A man can't live without his heart....Please! Make this go away." I didn't know he was talking about his death; I thought he was talking about his pain of living away from the family, without a home. Weeping myself, I told him, "I can't make it go away. We have lived together a long time and this is where it has led us. I have forgiven you too many times and I expected things to change. No! I can't do it anymore." After this, he left.

Much later, he came back. He seemed alright. He asked me if he could take the boys out and spend some time with them. He was very calm. He asked me if he would be allowed to see the boys in the future. I assured him that he was still their father and they still loved him; we could arrange it. He took them out for a while. Lee and I went to the store. When we came back the boys were at home and he was already gone. I felt relieved; things appeared to be leveling out and calming down. I thought, "Maybe he's just accepted this."

I didn't hear anything from him until Sunday morning. He again came to the house and let himself in. His footsteps woke me up. I jumped up and went to him. I told him, "You can't keep coming here, you don't live here anymore and you frighten me waking me up." Again, we went through the ordeal of his asking me to let him come back and my telling him why he couldn't. He began swinging from calm persuasion to suicidal threats. Then he got extremely angry. He finally said, "Okay, I am gonna go and I am gonna do it this time." He took off his ring and told me to give it to Wade. Then he gave me his wallet and his knife and walked out. He seemed so intent. I followed him outside. He had just given me his last will and testament. He had never done that before. I was crying and saying, "Please! Don't do this. Think about your children." It did not affect him.

He said, "Don't give me a funeral. My family (mother, sister, and brothers) doesn't love me and I don't want them to come and cry over my coffin and act like they loved me. They didn't want to see me when I was alive. Don't let them see me dead. You keep everyone away from me. Promise me."

I was trying to be assertive, repeating myself, "You can't do this, you have no right to do this, you have no right to do this to your children." He was saying, "You can stop me. All you have to do is to tell me I can stay." I was saying, "But you can't stay. You won't get help." It was my ultimate gamble. I was trying to force his hand.

He had talked about suicide so many times. I was interpreting it as his manipulation, his attempt to force me to take him back. And that's how it has always worked with the exception of his giving me his personal belonging and the expressed intent about the funeral. So I kept saying, "Please don't do this." Angrily he told me, "Well! I am going to. So, you might as well tell me good-by." Angry and crying, I said, "If you are that intent. If I have to tell you good-by, then good-by." That infuriated him; he said, "You bitch. You'll be getting a call from the hospital." He left. I was left with a very uneasy feeling. As soon as he left, I went in to the bedroom to see about the gun. It was gone. He must have gotten it before I woke up.

I called David. He was getting ready to leave his home and go to the funeral home to bury his father. In hindsight, that might have been what saved his life. I told him what had transpired through the week-end. He was incredulous but did take me seriously. He told me, "I'll watch out for him. Thank you for warning me."

I also called the police. I told them, "He has a gun now and I don't know where he has gone. He said something about the hospital." I think I said that but I am not sure. Events at this point are very blurred in my mind. I know I told them that he was staying with a friend of his, I described the part of the town his friend lived and I described the truck my husband was driving. The policeman told me that they would try to find him. Austin was gone for about thirty minutes when he called me from the lobby of the hospital and said, "I am getting ready to go out in the parking lot and shoot myself; but before I die, I want you to tell me one more time that you won't let me come back. Come to me and stop me."

He was so out of control that I was afraid of getting near him. What had already occurred on Friday had made me realize, "He could just snap and kill me." I felt he was at that point, of killing me. I told him, "No! I won't meet you there. You go in the Emergency Room, you see a doctor and you tell them what you're thinking. Please get help....Let them help you." He said with so much pain, "Nobody can help me." I told him, "Please let them try." I'd tried for years but I couldn't help him. I was tired. He said, "I should've known that you didn't care," and he hung up on me. Then he called me back after some time, very calm, telling me things that he wanted me to say to the children: how much he loved them; how proud he was of them, and it didn't have anything to do with them; that, it was just him. I was saying "Alright" after each of his statements. Then I said, "Please don't do this. If you love them, don't do this!" Again, I was met with this:

"You don't love me, or you would stop me." I tried to get him to tell me where he was but he wouldn't.

I wanted him to live. I wanted him to get help. I wanted him well. I would've gone to him but he wouldn't tell me where he was. Then he called me again. I was desperate but he wouldn't tell me where he was. He said, "Holly! This call is for you because I am about to die. Don't let anybody make you feel guilty. I know that people are going to blame you for it but I can't die without telling you that this isn't your fault and you don't have **anything** to feel guilty for." Then he said, "Because I know my mother, she will try to make you feel guilty. Don't let her. It didn't really have anything to do with you. It was my problem. I shouldn't ever have treated you that way. I'm sorry!" I tried to plead with him, "Please! don't do this." He said, "I love you Holly! Find yourself a nice man." He had never said those things to me before. In that instant, I knew he would die. But he wouldn't tell me where he was. I was crying. My last words to him were, "Get help." But he hung up the phone. I don't know if he even heard me.

At three minutes till noon, I got a call from a policeman. He was at the hospital. He said, "Come to the hospital's emergency room. Drive careful." I got there right after it had happened because his blood was still in the parking lot. It looked like gallons of blood. There were ground bits of bone and tissue, I thought it was his brain I was looking at. Even looking at his blood, I was thinking, "God! He can't be dead." He had been through serious injuries and he lived. He seemed immortal. I ran in. Stricken, I went to the nurses station, "Where is he! Where is he!" A nurse felt compassion. She put me in a room by myself and called my sister. Then two policeman came to me. The first thing I asked, "Is he alive?" They wouldn't say anything. They started asking me questions. I told them, "There isn't anything to tell." They asked me about the club he had in his truck. I told them, "He is paranoid." They asked where he got the gun. I said, "I've had you looking for him all morning." I noticed that they were talking about him in the past tense. Then they asked me if I wanted to see him. I told them "No. I don't want to see him."

He chose to live only for 66 hours without me. Now, his life was over. I was his heart. He had done what he had always told me he would do.

There are many things I don't remember about the days immediately after his death. It was a horror. I became so cold. I couldn't think. I couldn't believe what had happened. I mourned him. It was just terrible. His mother, as any mother would, initially blamed me. I could not accept condolences. I could barely speak. I was numb. I was protected by my relatives and friends. They were answering my door and screening my calls, buffering me from any further shocks. They spent the night and wouldn't let me be alone. I couldn't sleep. I realized how close I had been to death. I had seen my own death written in his eyes, but towards the end, it had worn my husband's face.

Ours had been a fight to the death. I went up to his coffin at the funeral home. His face that I had held so many times was so peaceful in death. The rage was gone. I talked to him in my mind. I was crying and I asked him, "Who won this fight, Austin?" I did not have a public viewing. I would not receive. But I did allow his family to tell him good-by.

When I buried him, that's when the terror became concrete. I remembered his father had told me once how much Austin was like their relative, the one, who I later found out had killed his wife. This relative believed that his wife had been going out on him. He killed his wife and killed himself. And, I realized I could have died too.

I had such terrible nightmares. I couldn't be in the dark. I dreaded to go to bed. The dream would always occur when I was falling asleep. I would hear his footsteps walking up on me in my sleep and I would wake up in terror. Then those terrible two and a half days would replay themselves in my mind. Sometimes, I wouldn't wake up; I would dream it all over again and it would become real again with all it's horror, the FEAR, the pain, the helplessness, and the blood.

David made the comment after Austin's death, "Who would have thought he was that way? He seemed so normal. He was such a good person."

This is a letter I wrote to Austin shortly after his death:

> *How do I begin this?*
>
> *By being dragged from sleep that you're here walking in this house, coming toward me.*
>
> *It finally became all to you, Austin...this disease with no name. I saw it's face through your raging features; but it's name...I need to know it's name.*
>
> *I want to be able to say, "It wasn't Austin who did these things, it was-----"*
>
> *Ultimately, you* **knew** *I was worthy. You entrusted me with your children.*
>
> *The pain and sorrow, was that part of it? Did you think about my pain, my children's pain? Were you buying their release and mine with your life's blood?*
>
> *What a horrible sadness you endured. Know that I helped you as much as I could for as long as I could. I know you realized that when you placed your benediction upon my head. I thank you for that. Such a typical act for you; an act of great kindness in the face of what you thought was a great betrayal on my part.*
>
> *You betrayed each one of us when you chose death. How could you choose death? That was your ultimate affirmation of love. That was your standard, that extreme, unreasoning, all consuming love. I am so sorry, Austin!*
>
> *We made a valiant effort, didn't we? I know you couldn't help it. I forgive you. You said, you wanted God to wrap His arms around you and hold you. I hope He has.*

IN RETROSPECT

Maybe things could have been different if I could have been more open with the counselor when I came alone to the clinic for help with my depression. But I was emotionally very vulnerable; I was under attack. I don't know if I could have said to the counselor that this man uses sex as a weapon against me. I am a private person and it would have been so embarrassing to say, "This man has raped me and I am still here. This man accuses me constantly of infidelity. This man has obtained sexual coercion through his manipulation. He has taken away my choices. He keeps me here with threats of death. But I love him!" How do you trust another person that much to say these things?

I was unable to present a clear picture because I didn't know what this disease was. His jealousy and his accusations only made me ashamed. He played on my guilt, though, there was no reason for me to feel guilty in the first place.

It is terribly embarrassing to talk about these things because you feel others would be asking in their mind, "Why? Why does she let him do this to her? She allows him. She's is a sick person. She must like it." After all it's a common assumption that it's a woman's fault. Furthermore, had I trusted the therapist enough to talk about it and had it not been handled correctly, it would have crushed me. I didn't think there was anybody out there in my situation. I thought no body would know about this kind of problem.

Austin once told me that he wanted his body donated to science. I am donating his mind to the behavioral sciences. He liked to help people. I wrote this for Austin. I loved the man he could have been, had he not been ravaged by this disease. I also wrote my story for the people who are even now living with this disease. I want to make a difference for the Austins and Hollys of the world.

JEALOUSY

Sabrina and Ashley's Dad and Holly's husband, had a "jealousy disorder" for which we chose to use the colloquial term "insane jealousy." A jealousy disorder may be with or without the DELUSION OF INFIDELITY. For our purpose, a jealousy disorder, without the delusion of infidelity is identified as "morbid jealousy" and the one with the delusion of infidelity, as "delusional jealousy." Delusion of infidelity means that a person has acquired a **fixed** and **false** belief that his partner is sexually unfaithful. A delusion is an unshakeable, obstinate belief which is not open to objective reasoning.

Sabrina and Ashley's Dad was delusionally jealous. To be very specific, in the general category of delusional jealousy, as will be defined later, he had a delusional disorder of jealousy. Here it would suffice to say that he did have a delusion of infidelity. A delusionally jealous person "sees" acts of adultery and unfaithfulness in normal and innocent day-to-day actions of the partner, such as the partner taking a shower, going to the yard, cleaning the yard, and other actions in similar daily events and occurrences.

A delusionally jealous person is hunting for a motive in a motiveless situation. Actions which should be taken at their face value acquire a sexual motive and meaning which point only in one direction and that is the direction of sexual unfaithfulness. For example, if she is taking a shower or doing her make up, it means she is getting ready to meet her lover, or she is trying to look more attractive, so she can seduce the men in the neighborhood. He is convinced of the acts of adultery although he does not have a reasonable cause for suspicion. His thinking, at least, in the area of his conjugal relationship, becomes highly distorted. A person with the delusion of infidelity can interpret virtually any action or event into a validation of his accusations. Innocent actions of the partner and common everyday events are interpreted as "evidence" of partner's infidelity. Delusions work with fantasy rather than with facts. A delusionally jealous person's faulty reasoning is foolproof, no ifs, ands, or buts are accommodated.

To draw a comparison, nondelusional jealousy, that is morbid jealousy, does not have equally inflexible and unshakeable false belief about the partner's unfaithfulness. Nor does it contain equally rigid and gross misinterpretation of daily routines and common actions of everyday life. Austin, Holly's husband, in our opinion, had a morbid jealousy disorder. Persons with nondelusional jealousy, at times, may be remorseful for making such accusations and suspecting the unfaithfulness of their partner. They may admit that they were wrong and promise to never repeat the behavior. Even when they are making accusations, they are aware, to some extent, of the possibility of their being wrong. They may occasionally think that they are being unfair to their partner in making such accusations. When confronted by another person, such as a relative, friend, or a therapist, they may concede that the basis of their suspicion has some loopholes and gaps. They cannot explain away all the facts and arguments presented by others to counter their reasoning.

Insane jealousy with or without the delusion of infidelity may be present in a number of mental disorders, such as, schizophrenia, psychotic mood disorders, organic mental disorders, and substance-abuse related disorders. There is a delusional disorder (paranoid disorder) which consists of delusional jealousy. In the psychiatric manual of diagnosis (DSM-III-R), it is referred to as "Delusional Disorder, jealousy type." It is a disorder in which the major problem is the delusion of infidelity. A delusional disorder can be highly elusive and difficult to detect. A person with a delusional disorder may not appear ill, unlike the patient with schizophrenia, manic-depressive illness, psychotic depression, or any other psychotic illness. Persons with a delusional disorder of jealousy may appear very normal at work, business, and social relations, at least to the outsiders. They can be highly rational and reasonable outside the area of spousal jealousy. They can be caring and concerned, or at least give the impression to others that they are. It is only in the relationship with their partner that the delusions are seen at work.

An extensive discussion of insane jealousy, delusion of infidelity, and other mental disorders associated with the jealousy disorder will follow after this chapter.

Jealousy can be of many forms. A person can be jealous of losing his coveted material possession, title or political position to another competitor. In this work, we are concerned with the "amorous jealousy." Amorous jealousy is also referred to, as "sexual jealousy," or "lover's jealousy."

Jealousy arises from the suspicion, apprehension, or knowledge that there is a rival. Jealousy is the fear of being supplanted in affection by a rival.

Jealousy is a negative emotion resulting from actual or threatened loss of love due to a rival. Jealousy stems from the distrust of the fidelity of one's partner or lover. A jealous person is harassed by the fear that he is being deceived by the person he loves and by another who is trying to supplant him in his beloved's heart.

In jealousy, a person believes that he is being deprived of that love, or that he is being replaced by another. The pain, in anticipation, or after the loss has occurred is about the loss of love or of the attention that he had been receiving. Jealousy is in direct proportion to the feeling of possession or ownership. The stronger the feeling of possession or ownership, the more intense is the feeling of jealousy. A jealous person is fearful of being replaced by another; he is fearful of losing his status as the sole and exclusive lover of his partner. He is alert and watchful of others lest he should lose this status to someone else. His emotional state is that of anger, fear and depression which can lead to violence. A person who is very prone or susceptible to the emotion of jealousy may be constantly entertaining thoughts along these lines, "It (he or she) is mine. I own it. It is rightfully mine. What is rightfully mine, let no one dare touch it."

Normal jealousy involves pain. It is a pain which results from the actual or feared loss of a loved person. However, it may be said, that in a person who is experiencing normal jealousy, his pain is normal but not rational. According to Freud, normal jealousy includes the following attributes:

Grief and **pain** caused by the thought of losing the loved object.

Hurt of self-pride and lowering of self-esteem.

Feelings of enmity against the successful rival. Please note that the enmity towards the rival is normal only when the rival has actually succeeded in conquering the loved object and not when it is only imaginary or anticipated. It is not normal to feel hostile towards an imagined rival.

Some measure of **self-criticism** as he holds himself responsible for the loss of his love.

Here, we would like to introduce the concept of healthy jealousy. What Freud called "rational jealousy," is akin to our concept of "healthy jealousy." Healthy jealousy must be derived from an actual situation. Jealousy cannot be called healthy if it is a product of a situation which involves an imaginary rival or an imagined loss. In other words, the loss is real and not a threatened loss. Furthermore, healthy jealousy must be proportionate to the threat posed by the real circumstances. An exaggerated or catastrophic response of grief or enmity is not permitted in a healthy jealousy. Also one's reactions should be under complete self-control. There is no reason for going berserk or going to pieces. In a healthy jealousy, a person's self-pride may be hurt when he loses his love to someone else but he does not hold anybody responsible for it. A person with healthy jealousy feels the pangs of jealousy and brushes them aside. He does not get obsessed with the idea of revenge. In the face of a threatened loss, he works on his relationship to improve what he can, to provide his best, but he does not try to unduly control or restrict his partner. He may even laugh at his feelings of jealousy. He does not imagine a rival when there is none.

Jealousy is an age-old emotion; it has been with us from the times man lived in the cave or formed the first tribal-social group. A Chief who had the first claim on food, women, and sleeping space, was the object of envy and jealousy of his tribesmen. He, in return, was suspicious and jealous of the young man whom he caught in a secret exchange of glance with the First Lady.

The word "jealousy" is derived from the Greek word "zelos" which means "zeal." Originally, jealousy, stood for fervor, warmth, ardor, desire, and the like. Therefore, in the early usage of the word, a "jealous" person was a "zealous" person. Jealousy was a noble passion and stood opposite of the emotion of "envy" which meant a malicious, spiteful, greedy desire for somebody else's possession.

Then, how did jealousy, from a noble passion, become a negative emotion?

Perhaps, many factors were responsible for this change. One reason could be that the Greek word "zelos" simply meant emulation or rivalry which by and large was in the tradition of a noble passion. However, rivalry could employ a number of positive or negative emotions directed towards the competitor. As the tradition would have it, the usage of "jealousy" in English language increasingly implied a negative emotion. Perhaps, unwittingly, jealousy was loaded up with negative emotions as part of a social defense against the severe emotion of envy. In my speculation, Englishmen, in their typical politeness and low-key approach, started referring to the ungentlemanly emotions such as malice, grudge, resentment, and the like, by the dubious label of "jealousy" rather than by the strong, tabooed label of "envy." In the German language, a distinction was maintained between the "good zeal" such as, ardor, emulation, and positive rivalry, and the "sick zeal" such as malice, envy, and avarice.

JEALOUSY AND ENVY

Jealousy and envy are mentioned in close context, and often compared and contrasted. At one time, as mentioned earlier, envy was a bad emotion while jealousy a neutral or a positive emotion. Envy is derived from the word, "invidere which means "to look maliciously upon," or to "cast an evil eye upon" another person. Therefore envy originally meant to look maliciously or spitefully at another person for his or her power, possessions, physical assets, personal qualities, etc. Needless to say that one only envies another person when one feels the envied person is superior, or has greater power, wealth, stronger physique, etc. The person who envies is greedy for those qualities, wants to take them away from the person he is envying and possess them for himself. An envious person resents and begrudges the envied person. Envy involves the wish to injure, to harm, and to rob the person of his envied possessions. Envy involves hate and resentment towards the envied person. Due to the involvement of negative emotions of hate, anger, resentment, and the like, envy was considered as major a sin as avarice or greed. But, as time went on, envy became a more socially acceptable word than did the word jealousy.

To reiterate the contrast, jealousy was a positive emotion of friendly rivalry and emulation, while envy was an evil emotion. It consisted of a malicious desire to possess something which belonged to somebody else. Logically, then, envy should have received increasingly greater disapproval. So, how come jealousy got the worse deal? Well, we can only speculate. Perhaps, in those times, to sugarcoat the not-so-honorable feelings of envy, we began to refer to them as jealousy.

Therefore, over a period of time, jealousy acquired the connotation of fear, distrust, pain and similar other feelings related with losing something of one's own to somebody else. Carrying that line of thinking further, I reason that as negative connotations of envy were piggybacked on jealousy, it became socially acceptable to label one's desire of grabbing or snatching something from another person as "envy."

What is the difference between envy and jealousy today, or are they interchangeable?

This is one of the most frequently asked questions in the context of jealousy. From the professional point of view, there is a distinction between these two terms. However, in common parlance, the distinction between these two terms has increasingly blurred and is now almost extinct. People use it interchangeably as an adjective: "I am envious of you," or "I am jealous of you". For using the verb, people have no choice but to use the verb "envy." For example, we say, "I envy you," we can't grammatically say, "I jealousy you."

There is an important distinction between envy and jealousy which would be useful to maintain in common usage. We are "envious" of a person who possesses something that we do not, but, we are "jealous" of him who might take away what we already possess. In envy, we covet something which we do not yet have. In jealousy, we fear losing something we already have. Jealousy happens to the owner of a possession or property. He feels he owns it and fears that someone is trying to take it away from him, or someone has already denuded him of his possession. Jealousy is more acute when one feels that not only is the thief trying to steal his possession or property but also, it (his woman) is walking away from him towards the thief. It may be said that jealousy is an emotion of "Haves" and envy is an emotion of "Have-nots."

Jealousy invariably involves three people, the lover, the beloved, and the rival. On the other hand, envy takes just two persons, the one who has "it" (the enviable possession) and the other who doesn't.

Albeit the differences, complex as our emotions are, there is almost always an interplay of jealousy and envy. In most of the cases, where there is jealousy, there is envy. A person who is jealous of another, if the latter should win favors of his beloved, must also feel he is lacking something in his own self. A jealous person is envious, consciously or subconsciously, of the charm and attributes he feels his rival has and he is lacking. It may be said that jealousy and envy are two sides of the same coin.

JEALOUSY AND CULTURAL EXPRESSIONS

One way of understanding a psychological characteristic or an emotion is to look at the various expressions, phrases, and idioms in that culture that refer to it. Such cultural expressions can lead to a historical and current understanding of a particular emotion or psychological characteristic. Cultural expressions and usages in reference to jealousy are numerous.

Did you know that the Venetian blinds are called "jealousies"? What could possibly be the connection between jealousy and Venetian blinds?

An important ingredient of jealousy is watching one's turf. In extreme cases, watching becomes spying. The connection between secret watching and jealousy was identified several hundred years ago. The evidence of this connection is present in the Venetian blinds. That connection is over four hundred years old. In Italy, the word "gelosia" is used for Venetian blinds from the 16th century. Since the 17th century, the French call Venetian blinds, jalousie. The choice of the name of jalousie seems to have originated in an amusing thought someone entertained about the Venetian blinds: A jealous husband or lover could watch his beloved, unnoticed and out of everyone's sight, behind those shutters. In English, "jealousy" for Venetian blinds entered in the early 19th century. In modern French literature, there is an interesting reference to the practice of secret watching by a jealous person. Alain Robbe Grillet in "La Jalousie" (1957), portrays a jealous husband who constantly watches the actions of his wife and her suspected lover through a jalousie.

How does the color "green" come to be the color of jealousy? Are there any other colors associated with jealousy?

In literature, jealousy is associated with specific colors. Someone "turns green with envy (or jealousy)." Jealousy is called the "green eyed monster." In Swedish and Norwegian languages, it is the color black that is associated with jealousy. Each association of color and jealousy has an interesting story to tell.

The word for jealousy-stricken, in Swedish and Norwegian languages, is svartsjuk. Svart means black and sjuk means sick. So, literally, "jealousy stricken" is "black sick." One reason for the association of black with jealousy could be that there is a certain amount of sadness and grief in jealousy, and black is typically associated with sadness, loss, and grief. Another reason may lie in the Norwegian tradition of courtship. In the Scandinavian countries, it was customary for the rejected suitor to put on black stockings after refusal from the prospective bride. This clearly pointed out to all parties concerned that the courtship for that suitor was over. Why did black stockings mean that the courtship was over? Well, for that one has to look up another Norwegian tradition. According to this tradition, a suitor wore green stockings when he was courting. This very perceptible switch from green to black stockings was a good social code as it clearly indicated where all the vying males stood with regard to the prospective bride. But sometimes what is good for the goose is not good for the gander. That fine custom made the wearer of black stockings, "black sick", that is "svart sjuk." However, in this tradition, one can also see the connection between the color green and jealousy. There is a Danish-Norwegian proverb, "make one's stockings green" which meant to court somebody. Therefore, when the winners or the one still-in-the-race, wear green stockings and the losers wear black stockings, it is easy to understand why they turn "green with jealousy."

Another association of jealousy with the color green originates from Shakespeare's classic phrase, "green- eyed monster." In Othello, Iago, the flag bearer, says to the Noble Moor, Othello:

O, beware, my lord, of jealousy;
It is the green-eyed monster which doth mock
the meat it feeds on.

The green-eyed monster that Shakespeare had in mind refers to cats, tigers, and other animals of feline species which first play with their victims before they kill them. Jealousy, too, plays with its victims who are in its grasp before it consumes them. A person, who is insanely jealous, dies hundreds of deaths from humiliation in the imaginary hands of the winning lovers. Furthermore, the metaphor of green-eyed monster has an interesting psychological connotation; jealousy, especially the insane jealousy, brings out the primitive and animal-like emotions in human beings.

JEALOUSY IN RELIGION

The emotion of jealousy, in Biblical times, was put on a divine pedestal. That may be one of the reasons why some people even take pride in being jealous. The divine jealousy is called "Godly jealousy." The essence of exclusive loyalty and divine jealousy is found in the following passage of the Old Testament (New American Standard Bible):

You shall not worship them or serve them (other gods); for I, the Lord your God, am a jealous God,....
(Exodus 20:5)

It conveys in no uncertain terms that Godly jealousy tolerates no unfaithfulness or defection. It demands exclusive worship and love. The jealous God is intolerant of disloyalty or infidelity and is absolutely autocratic. It was taught that unfaithfulness was so unbearable that it made God wrathful and ready for vengeance. Stories were told to instill fear in the minds of the followers by themes of vengeance God wreaked on them who showed a divided loyalty and made God jealous and vengeful. The churches and the religious authorities played on these human fears to demand unfailing commitment and unswerving loyalty to one God.

It seems that in the state of insane jealousy, human beings start acting like gods; they demand exclusive worship and love from their spouses and tolerate no unfaithfulness, imagined or feared though it may be on their part. When the jealousy gets the better of them, they become intolerant even of the suggestion of disloyalty. They demand unquestionable and unwavering faithfulness. They either obsessively wish or actually seek revenge for all acts of disloyalty or attraction to anyone else. It seems that the themes of unfaithfulness and revenge are stored deep in our psyche. More will be coming later on these themes when we discuss the topic of infidelity.

An intensely jealous person is suspicious and apprehensive of a potential rival. He protects his turf aggressively. He watches his property and possessions. He is resentfully envious and demands exclusive loyalty from other people. If these qualities and behaviors are present to an extreme degree in a person, then we have an insanely jealous person on our hands.

INFIDELITY AND ADULTERY

We in a male dominated society have carried some extreme and irrational ideas about infidelity and adultery. Such ideas and attitudes clearly disfavor women and justify violence and control of a woman in the mind of a jealous man. It is time to understand the laws and customs that are based on these prejudiced ideas and attitudes, the purpose of which is to serve masculine pride and protect male interests.

Discovery of adultery is considered such an extreme provocation that it justifies even the severe form of male violence in the judgement of many. Sexual intercourse between a married woman and a man other than her husband amounted to a sin and a crime. Infidelity was and it still is a cardinal sin. It threatens a man's monopoly and all his sexual and property rights he deems he has over a woman. Besides, it severely bruises his masculine pride. Jealousy is a special product of the patriarchal system. Kings, Dukes, and Eastern Nabobs could have hundreds of women as their wives or concubines but if any one of those women was ever suspected of a sexual relation with another man, she and the suspected transgressor met their fatal end. Soldiers put the chastity belt on their wives to prevent any possible transgressions but freely plundered the women of the conquered lands.

In the majority of societies, such as many of the Asian, European, and Middle Eastern societies, a sexual act between a man and a woman was labelled as an act of "adultery" if the woman was a married woman. It did not create any ripples, nor was it castigated as adultery if a married man entered into an extra-marital affair as long as the woman was not married.

It is actually in the twentieth century that the laws against adultery, at least legally speaking, were enacted which would apply equally against men and women. During the French revolution, in the 19th century, "tougher" laws were made against male adultery. How tough were these laws? French revolutionary laws made it a crime for a man to keep a concubine if it was against his wife's wishes!

Many societies justified a man's rage and even violence if his wife had committed adultery. According to a Texan Law, if a man personally saw his wife in the actual act of adultery and if he instantly killed his wife, sexual transgressor, or both, he would have received no legal consequences because such an act was not considered a crime. Many times, in the bargain pleas or in the appeals in the U.S. courts, a murder is reduced to manslaughter if it was a result of "provocation" in view of the wife's act of adultery. However, according to some experts of law, it is doubtful if the courts and the jury would be as sympathetic to a homicidal wife as they would to a homicidal husband.

Even, in the courts which recognize adultery-related killing as a criminal offense, judges and jury tend to treat a husband's jealous rage with sympathy resulting in lighter sentences for the crime. It seems implicit in these unwritten laws and social attitudes that it is human nature, or specifically, the nature of man to become violent or even commit homicide when provoked by adultery.

LOVE AND HEALTHY JEALOUSY

Human nature is not animal nature. It is time to free ourselves from such gross misconceptions and erroneous conclusions about human nature. It is not human nature to be violent. It is not human nature to be utterly possessive of one's beloved person. Intense jealousy does not mean love. Controlling another person by force, threat or coercion is not love. A slave in bondage can fear and obey but cannot love his or her captor. As a matter of fact, animals do not captivate or terrorize their mates. For emotionally mature human beings, love is a matter of choice and not compulsion. Love means setting free and letting the other person choose to love out of his or her own free will. True love can only exist between the two equal partners, it can never survive between the dominant and the dominated. True love could only be between persons who respect each other. Do you respect your partner? If not, it is most doubtful that you truly love your partner.

Jealousy only breeds jealousy. Jealousy destroys the love that it tries to save. If you are jealous of your partner, let go of your jealousy. Healthy jealousy means that if you perceive a threat of loss of your partner's affection, you do not get angry or blame your partner or the potential rival. In a healthy jealousy, you understand that the fear and pain you experience is entirely your problem and your problem alone. You even laugh at your self for being jealous. Do not lead yourself to believe that it is your partner's fault or somebody else's fault that you feel so rotten. Shake off that feeling of jealousy before it gets a hold on you. Think of the reasons why you could be wrong in what you are suspecting. Think of the reasons why your hunch may be wrong.

Trust in an intimate relationship is an internal feeling; you on the inside feel you can or can't trust that person. Nothing will be gained by keeping a close tab on the partners, spying on them, or by imposing restrictions on their movements and actions. If you feel your partner is taking extraordinary interest in another person or you suspect your partner is cheating on you, discuss that calmly and in a straightforward manner. If you feel the problem still persists, insist on getting professional help for you and your partner.

If your partner wants some breathing space and time to think things over, permit the space to your partner graciously.

If your partner does not feel the same attraction and love for you anymore, walk away rather than pleading, begging, or threatening your partner. You cannot revive or gain anymore love by imposing yourself.

SYMPTOMS AND BEHAVIORS IN THE
DISORDERS OF JEALOUSY

Insane jealousy is the excessive preoccupation with sexual unfaithfulness of the spouse and marked intolerance of potential rivals. Once the intensity of insane jealousy is modified, insanely jealous persons may be remorseful for making such accusations and suspecting the faithfulness of the partner. They may admit that they were wrong and promise to never repeat the behavior. In the less severe state of insane jealousy, that is, morbid jealousy, even when they are making accusations, they are aware of the possibility of their being wrong and they may occasionally think that they are being unfair to their spouse in making such accusations. When confronted by a relative, friend, or a therapist, they may concede that the basis of their suspicion has some loopholes and gaps. In the more severe state of insane jealousy, that is delusional jealousy, there are no doubts recast by the jealous partner and no remorse experienced.

Insane jealousy is a colloquial term. Insane jealousy occurs with or without the delusion of infidelity. Insane jealousy without the delusion of infidelity is the less severe form, referred to as morbid jealousy. Insane jealousy with the delusion of infidelity, the more severe form of insane jealousy, is referred to as delusional jealousy. A condition in which the only significant problem is the delusion of infidelity, and it is not caused by any chemical, physical-organic or mental disorder, is called a "delusional disorder of jealousy." We will first describe the signs and symptoms of morbid jealousy. We will then describe the characteristics of the delusion of infidelity so that you can recognize it when you see one.

SIGNS OF INSANE JEALOUSY WITHOUT THE DELUSION OF INFIDELITY

(MORBID JEALOUSY)

These signs may be found in morbid jealousy as well as delusional jealousy. One sign alone does not prove the presence or absence of insane jealousy. It is more reliable to look for a combination of signs. For a more complete understanding of delusional jealousy, you are advised to also review the section on delusional jealousy.

A person is insanely jealous if he exhibits several of the following behaviors:

1. **Extreme Moodiness.** He shows emotional immaturity and belligerence. At times, he is in a good mood, cuts up and displays good humor. Other times, he is withdrawn, unpredictable, displays inappropriate rage and mood swings. Mood swings are related to the rage he experiences towards the partner.

2. **Extreme Quietness.** He will not say or answer anything, leaving family members at a loss as to what to do or say. At such times, he is withdrawn from his partner and others. Members of the family have to somehow figure out some way of approaching him without his getting enraged. In spite of all their efforts, they may not always be successful in keeping his rage from being set off. These periods of quietness are cyclical and concurrent with accusatory behavior. His ability to handle stress is almost zero at these times. As some family members describe it, "It is like walking on egg shells around him."

3. **Watching and Monitoring.** He watches and monitors his partner's actions and movements closely. When his partner is around another person, he pays even closer attention to everything being said or done. He can separate comments out of context and elaborate them in a way that would give them a totally new meaning. He might end up deriving

something totally sinister of an innocent remark. Deep distrust is exhibited at such times. Also, he may feel he is the object of derision and humor by his partner's friends and relatives which compel him to further watch and monitor his partner when others are around.

4. **Keeps the partner right under his nose.** He doesn't trust his partner out of his sight. He is extremely suspicious of even short absences and distances. He wants his partner where he can watch her, touch her and make absolutely sure that nothing can possibly take place behind his back.

5. **Spies on the partner.** He can use devious ways to spy on his partner. He may hire a private detective, bug the phone, regularly search her pocket book and all personal possessions, and secretively solicit help of some relatives to keep an eye on his partner. He may take a temporary leave from home to go to a hide-out, to give the impression to his partner that she has a free hand for the time being, and come back surreptitiously to spy on her movements.

6. **Believes he is of no worth or interest to the partner.** He feels that his partner has lost interest in him or he was never of much significance or interest to his partner. Negative feelings and low self-esteem may be apparent in his statements, for example, "I am not such a hunk like your friends you fancy. I guess I am not good enough for you." He suspects that the partner's sexual interests are placed elsewhere. He feels that she has lost interest in him because of her lustful actions elsewhere. He thinks that she has an extraordinary sexual appetite or preferences which cannot be satisfied by normal means, so she is going elsewhere to satisfy her aberrations.

7. **Expresses jealousy towards the partner.** He feels that wherever she goes, she becomes the center of attraction. He may express some resentment in hearing comments from others, such as, "Oh! she is very pretty," or "She is smart while making conversation," or, "Every one in the office loves her." He is jealous of her, feeling that she has all those qualities to steal the show and draw everybody's attention. He feels left out. He may be heard making statements, such as, "You are pretty, so everybody wants to grab you. They are not interested in me. They come here for you. Do you think, I don't know that?"

8. **Intolerant of friends or relatives.** He doesn't want his partner to have any close friend of either sex. If they have a friendship with another couple, it soon comes to an end. Friends and relatives are accused of trying to break up the relationship between him and his spouse. He perceives them as a threat to his exclusive relationship.

9. **Intolerant of compliments to his partner.** He doesn't like anyone to compliment the partner on her looks or any qualities. He doesn't want his partner to look nice in clothes or put on make up. If the partner looks particularly attractive in some nice clothing, she may be forbidden to wear it. Clothes may be shredded to pieces, her hairdo may have to be undone, and make up may have to be washed. He is suspicious of her motivation for grooming. He believes she is trying to be seductive for not so honorable a purpose.

10. **Intolerant of affection or attention expressed towards his partner by others.** He is extremely jealous of his partner receiving any affection or attention even from her own parents, siblings and female friends. He can't tolerate the partner receiving love even from her own children.

11. **Sudden and enexpected outbursts of rage related to jealousy.** Sometimes, the suddenness and abruptness of these eruptions take the partner and other family members by surprise. They cannot understand what exactly causes so much anger or where it is coming from. They say, "His face changes. His eyes look frightening at such time." Some describe him as a Jekyll and Hyde type person who is extremely charming and demonstrative towards the partner, but in the context of insane jealousy, he suddenly transforms into a roaring, raging, assaultive person. Another Jekyll and Hyde-type person described by a nonjealous partner is one who seems very confident and assured in public but, privately, in relation to his partner, he is extremely possessive, controlling, and insecure.

12. **Doubts his partner's faithfulness without reason or basis .** Just her talking to a person of the opposite sex may trigger off suspicions regarding her unfaithfulness.

13. **Questions with intense severity about the time spent in his or her absence.** His partner has to provide the smallest details. He repeats his questions to check if she gives a

different answer. He cross checks the details to investigate if she is lying.

14. **Questions scathingly about his partner's amorous relationships with people at work.** Besides questioning her, he may drop in at her work without letting her beforehand so he can check if she is acting friendly with her male colleagues. He may phone her at work at different hours to check if she is out of her office without his knowledge.

15. **Relentless and untiring questioning on the nature of his partner's premarital relationships,** or of previous relationships if the couple is unmarried. It seems, he really wants to get every possible detail of the sexual acts in the premarital relations: How often did you go to bed with him? How many times did you go to bed altogether? Was he better than I? If his partner says that she did not have sex with her pre-marital friend, he refuses to believe it, "Yes, you did. Stop telling me lies."

16. **Keeps close track of his partner's time, travel, and pocket money.** This is done to verify if she is up to any sexual misbehavior with her lovers. Keeping a tab on the partner is described in detail in the section, "Domestic Espionage."

17. **Directly accuses his partner of unfaithful behavior.** He may claim that he has direct knowledge of such a behavior. To a partner who has been faithful, such accusations come as a total shock. In insane jealousy with delusion of infidelity, accusations may be graphic and too far-fetched. He may even accuse the relatives of his partner's family of incest with his partner.

18. **Insistent demanding of confession from his partner of sexual misconduct.** He insists that she give up her "bad ways" and confess, so that the correction of the misconduct can begin. An insanely jealous person with a delusion of infidelity becomes desperate for confession. He not only demands it, he tries to extract it. For further information, refer to the section on Delusion of Infidelity.

19. **Becomes angry if his false beliefs about unfaithfulness are challenged.** The anger seems to result from his frustration that whatever chance there was for correction of the misconduct is thinning away because no one seems to recognize the seriousness of the problem.

20. **Abusive and assaultive behavior towards the partner.** He feels threatened and enraged, suspecting that the partner

is still engaged in the misconduct and thus causing him humiliation. Often, violence occurs if he is a product of machomania and has little respect for women. In some cases assault may also occur towards the suspected rival. Although less frequently, women also become violent in their spells of insane jealousy.

21. **Disallows the partner from all outside contact and communication,** such as from going out, picking up mail, receiving phone calls, etc. He places restrictions on his partner's contact even with close relatives and friends. He does not allow partner to take trips on her own. Controlling behavior may be camouflaged with flattering statements, "I just want to be close to you." He doesn't want his partner to go anywhere without him. If his partner goes anywhere on her own, he requires an account of everything done or said while she was away.

22. **Doubts the paternity of his own children.** Sometimes insane jealousy "explodes" on the partner for the first time when she breaks the news of her pregnancy. It is at this point that she finds out the extent of jealousy and the suspicion that was brewing in his mind. He may not continuously disbelieve that he is the father of children. The doubt may revive now and then, especially, when insane jealousy becomes dominant. If the doubts about paternity come up after an affair is unearthed, especially, around the time of conception, that does not signify insane jealousy. The uncertainty about the fatherhood of their child is a problem that is specific to men. They have no way of being certain of their fathering a child except by their own trust in their partner. Needless, to say that women do not doubt the maternity of their children unless they are in a grossly psychotic state .

23. **Believes that his partner is oversexed.** Since he believes that his partner is constantly making sexual transgressions indiscriminately, he explains it by another false belief that she has an extraordinary appetite for sex. In some cases, it provides him a justified excuse to perpetrate rather perverted sexual behaviors in an attempt to satisfy her supposedly abnormal craving for sex.

24. **Other suspicions.** Some morbidly jealous persons may suspect that their partners are going to harm them or get rid of them or that their partners have developed a venereal

disease. However, those may be suspicions and not firm beliefs. For more details, refer to the section on Delusional Jealousy.

DELUSION OF INFIDELITY

(DELUSIONAL JEALOUSY)

What is a delusion?

A delusion is a false or unreasonable idea. However, people who have a delusion, do not see their delusion as being a false or unreasonable idea. In fact they see it as the absolute truth and others can't change their belief about it by reasoning or logic. If you produce one argument to prove that their belief is illogical or false, they are likely to produce a counter argument to prove that you are wrong. Delusion is a part of the mind that is set in concrete. You may also say that a delusion is a mind set. It is an unshakeable, inflexible belief that remains unchanged by normal logic and reasoning. This belief becomes established in the mind of a deluded person as a foolproof fact. He may have experiences which to others may show that his belief is baseless; but he fails to see where his belief falls short of reality.

What is a delusion of infidelity?

A person with the delusion of infidelity is convinced without due cause that his or her partner is unfaithful. A normal person would not carry such a conviction without due cause being available to him. Questioning someone's faithfulness is serious business. Therefore, one would expect that before charges of infidelity are made, the accuser has carefully checked the facts and weighed the evidence before making such a serious charge. But in the delusion of infidelity, that is hardly the case. With patently false judgment and illogical deductions, a person reaches the conclusion that his or her spouse is unfaithful. These conclusions are derived from simple everyday events, such as her looking out of the window, going out to the yard, or wearing decent clothes. These everyday behaviors are taken as positive proof of her unfaithfulness. The basis of his claims of deception by the partner and his reasoning of arriving at that conclusion from her innocent behavior are preposterous. His repeated conclusions, over a period of time, become his firm and fixed beliefs of his partner's unfaithfulness. These beliefs are unshakeable and unchangeable by reasoning or persuasion.

A question is often raised as to how does one know what is "real" and what is "delusional?" Mental health professionals often ask, "How do I know he is delusional, maybe his spouse is unfaithful? These things happen all the time, don't they?" The answer is that whether the accused spouse is faithful or not is really irrelevant to the question of whether a person is delusional or not. To determine if the ideas of unfaithfulness are delusional or not, one has to look at how the jealous person arrives at that conclusion. A delusional person does not conclude that his partner is unfaithful by the normal tools of reasoning. The evidence he produces in support of his delusion is based on trivial and common day occurrences. If a person with normal and logical reasoning observes the same thing, he would not jump to such a conclusion. In fact, if a reasonable person weighs the "evidence" presented by a delusional person, he will dismiss it immediately and entirely. He would pronounce the judgment of "Non sequitur, "It does not follow." He would conclude that the premise of the argument does not prove anything.

The delusion of infidelity physically involves another person. Other delusions, at times, are contained within the person and do not lend themselves to harm any other person. For example, the delusion that "I am Jesus," or "My intestines are rotting," may trouble the person but has little potential of harming other people. However, the delusion of infidelity torments the deluded individual and leads to abusive behavior and violence against another person, the victim-partner. Therefore, the delusion of infidelity not only tells us that the delusional person is suffering from a mental illness but also that someone else's health may be in danger.

Signs and symptoms of delusional jealousy, by and large, are not drastically different from morbid jealousy; they are just more severe and intense in delusional jealousy. In the section, "Signs of Insane Jealousy Without The Delusion Of Infidelity," the behaviors that are described may apply to morbid jealousy as well as delusional jealousy. You may first like to review the behaviors listed in "Signs of Insane Jealousy..." and then review this section to sharpen the understanding of delusional jealousy. Again, presence or absence of one sign alone does not determine delusional jealousy. It is more reliable to look for a combination of the behaviors described below. Here is a description of behaviors that are observed in the delusion of infidelity:

1. **Obsession with premarital relationship of his partner.** He unceasingly asks questions to his spouse about the sexual aspects of her premarital relationships.

These questions embarrassingly probe into the minute details of the sexual behavior. It is evident that the questioner is getting some pleasure out of the intimate questions. He disbelieves the partner who, truthfully, did not have any sexual relationship with the person in question. But such denials from the victim-partner make him even more distrustful of her.

In morbid jealousy, questioning of the premarital relationships may be persistent and embarrassing to the partner, but may not reach the intensity of an obsession as is the case with the delusion of infidelity.

2. **Intense preoccupation with his partner's sexual behavior and infidelity.** This becomes an obsession and occupies most of his time of actual interaction with his partner. He severely cuts down on his social and occupational activities in the outside world and spends maximum possible time with the partner to prevent her from the possible sexual misconduct. He is constantly asking, "Who were you with? What is the name of your lover? What sexual acts were involved?" Unfortunately, some spouses see this as a sign of love and put up with it as a necessary evil.

3. Tries to extract confession of imagined misconduct from his innocent partner. He really becomes desperate to get a confession. Note that he does not simply demand a confession, he tries to extract it. In morbid jealousy, the jealous person wants the nonjealous partner to confess but he is not desperate to get it. It appears that a delusional jealous person is seeking for reassurance that he is not imagining things and that the unfaithfulness is real. Often, in such cases, his conscious reasoning is that if she goes ahead and confesses it, then there is a hope for her; her misconduct may be corrected. However, it is possible that a delusional person is vaguely anxious that he is loosing his mind. A confession, forced though it may be, would reassure him that the infidelity is all real, he did not imagine it and he is not going crazy. However, her refusal to confess (and why should she if she has not done any wrong!) strengthens his belief that she does not want to reform herself. Unfortunately, it is one of the saddest "catch-22" situations.

4. Becomes infuriated if his false beliefs about unfaithfulness are challenged. He tries desperately to confirm his beliefs by investigating the most trivial matters. He takes them to the limits of absurdity. He is consumed by the need to prove the acts of infidelity. He sees evidence everywhere. Therefore, when the basis of his delusions is questioned, it is seen as an enemy action. He accuses the challenger of taking side with his partner and disbelieving him. A morbidly jealous person does not so vigorously or vehemently quarrel with the challenge to his belief as a delusional person would. Since the former does not have a delusion, he does not have so much energy to invest in his claim. Further, a morbidly jealous person, for the sake of argument, may accept the possibility that he could be wrong in his assumption of his partner's unfaithfulness, but a delusionally jealous person would not. He may even promise the therapist to "shut off his mind" from such thoughts and to believe "her innocence for the time being." A delusionally jealous person may come to do that only after considerable progress in the treatment.

5. Excessive anger, rage, and hate towards his partner for being unfaithful. A delusional person has "moods" or spells of rage, suspicions, and accusations for a period of time,

days, weeks, or months, and then it subsides only to return
with greater intensity in the next "mood."
Incidents of outrage and assaultive behavior, one time or
another do occur. Violent assaults stem from accusations of
infidelity.   Over a period of time, they happen more
frequently and increase in intensity.   A morbidly jealous
person does not feel so strongly convinced in his mind of the
unfaithfulness of the partner and thereby he may feel guilty
for the violence towards the partner. A delusionally jealous
person is furious with the partner for being so "cruel" to him
and for "abusing" the marriage. He sees the violent acts as
"just punishment," or "deterrents" to the abuse of marital
trust. See below, the "Lack of remorse for accusations and
violence."

6. **The idea of unfaithfulness has an abnormal charge.**   Even
in a calm state of mind, or inactive stage of delusional
jealousy, if the topic of partner's unfaithfulness is broached,
the insanely jealous person becomes agitated and enraged.
His emotions start getting out of control, he shakes in rage,
his eyes begin to emit fire, his face becomes red hot, and he
begs you not to ask him anything more about it. The change
of emotional state in the jealous individual is so dramatic
and incredible that some family members describe him as
having a "double personality"; as if, in the state of jealousy,
another person, a total "stranger," in contrast of the character
of the person, takes over. This change is somewhat similar
to the Jekyll and Hyde phenomenon described in morbid
jealousy, but only more scary and real.

7. **Lack of remorse for accusations or violence towards his
partner.**   Any violence or fury unleashed in response to a
delusion of unfaithfulness is beyond reproach or guilt. A
delusional person does not apologize for this act. He does
not feel remorseful for his accusations of unfaithfulness, for
physical assaults, or angry outbursts. On the contrary, he
feels quite justified in his actions. For instance, a nonjealous woman, after an episode of jealous rage of her
partner, thought that he was making overtures to her. She,
in the act of forgiving, asked him if he felt sorry for hitting
her. His face and his demeanor changed immediately and he
said, "You should thank your stars because it could have
been worse."

8. **Goes to great lengths in monitoring his partner's movements and actions.** It is not just a matter of keeping an eye on the partner, his obsession with watching her is total. There are instances in which delusionally jealous individuals have left their jobs to keep a 24-hour vigil on their partner. In morbid jealousy, keeping track of partner's movements, actions, time, travel, bank accounts, and spending may not be so tight and preoccupying as it is in delusional jealousy.

9. **Attempts to severely control movements and interaction of his partner with others.** Delusionally jealous persons try and often succeed in restricting the most legitimate and essential movements of the victim-partner. For example, they don't even let their partner see the doctor for physical illness in the fear that she would take that opportunity for initiating sexual misconduct, maybe with the physician. Especially, if it is a visit to a male Ob-Gyn, he would make it sure that he accompanies his partner, and if he can help it, he would like to be physically present in the examination room.

10. **Gross misinterpretations and misperceptions.** His claims of deception by his partner are based on a gross misinterpretation of everyday life activities, trivial events, and common occurrences. For example, her going to the bathroom, standing in the yard, sitting sideways, wearing her make up and similar other actions, don't just cast a doubt in his mind, they are sure "evidence" of her unfaithful behavior. A person with morbid jealousy does not show such a gross misinterpretation. For example, a morbidly jealous partner may see his partner talking to another man in a faultlessly social situation and he may suspect that an affair is going on between the two. However, a delusionally jealous person does not have to see his partner talking to another man. He may reach that conclusion by merely noticing the way she was standing by herself at a particular time of the day. It is for this reason that many delusionally jealous partners cannot give a definite identification or specific personal details of the potential suspects; they refer to the rivals as "all those men" or "whoever they are." Misinterpretations are generally of the visual content, that is, he tends to misinterpret more of what he **sees** rather than of what he **hears**. However, at times, he grossly misinterprets

what he hears, although not as frequently as with visual misinterpretations.

11. **Disputes the paternity of children.**   He argues and refuses to acknowledge that he is the real father of the children. However, in some cases, when the child grows up and comes to have an undeniable resemblance to his jealous father, he drops his protestation. However, this may still not make a dent in his delusion that she is unfaithful to him. In morbid jealousy, a person may doubt the paternity of his children but may not be so adamant in his disbelief of the true paternity of the children.   Some morbidly jealous persons may believe that the partner is unfaithful but not dispute the paternity of the children. These guidelines are only applicable in absence of a discovery of an extra-marital affair.   In the knowledge of an actual unfaithful behavior, especially around the time of conception, true paternity may be highly suspected even in nonjealous partners.

12. **Believes that his partner is a sex maniac.** He is convinced that his partner is oversexed, and is surely a pervert with insatiable sexual hunger. He may call his female partner a "nympho." He may believe that his partner craves for sex several times a day from several people. His belief that no one man can satisfy her validates in his mind his accusations that she is running around with other men.   The female partner is forced to act very carefully, lest she comes on to the jealous partner initiating sex or desiring sex. Such an overture on her part would be a confirmation for him of his belief that she is truly a nymphomaniac.

A morbidly jealous person may have a similar hypersexual view of his partner, but a delusionally jealous person arrives at this conclusion in a delusional fashion. For example, as a delusionally jealous person "sees" that she goes to the bathroom frequently, holds her body tight, or perspires profusely, he "knows" that she is overindulging in sex or has an insatiable sexual craving.

13.   **Excessive effort to sexually saturate his partner.**   It stems from the belief that his partner has an abnormal sexual drive. He makes a desperate attempt to prevent her from indulging in sexual indiscretions elsewhere. This is a rationalization on his part. Perhaps, he himself has an extraordinary sexual appetite and hidden perversions which he cannot admit to himself or acknowledge that he wants to

act on such forbidden desires for his own pleasure. Since he has come to have a belief that she is a nymphomaniac, he feels compelled to keep her "satisfied." In this manner, he can satisfy his own perverted desires without consciously accepting them as his own.

14. **Believes that his partner has a venereal disease.** Many delusionally jealous persons come to believe that their partners, due to their own fault (of indiscreet sexual behavior), are infected with a venereal disease or with some other horrific infectious disease. They, then, begin to be troubled by the thoughts that they are going to catch or have already caught a venereal disease from their sexually indiscriminate partner. Some of them may avoid having any sexual relations with their partner as a measure of self-protection. This may serve as a rationalization for the delusionally jealous person who is consciously or subconsciously troubled by his impotence.

15. **Fear of harm from his partner.** Many delusionally jealous persons develop an irrational fear that their partners are going to hurt them, or harm them or that they are conspiring with their lovers to simply get rid of them. They begin to fear that their partnesr are going to poison them, mixing something in their food, or do something to get them out of their way. Their reasoning for such an action by their partner may be along these lines, "She is trying to get rid of me so that she can run around with other men as she pleases."

In delusional jealousy, the motive is always the unfaithfulness. A similar fixed and false belief that someone is going to kill or harm the person, but without the motive of unfaithful behavior, is a delusion of persecution.

A morbidly jealous person may suspect that his partner is going to or might harm him but he does not seriously believe that the source of his fear is valid unless he has persecutory or some other type of delusion.

Also, at times, there is overlapping between various types of delusions. A delusion of infidelity may be accompanied by a persecutory delusion. The important difference to remember between delusional thinking and nondelusional thinking, for fear of harm from the partner, is that a nondelusional person suspects but the delusional person does not merely suspect, he believes that his partner is going to harm him.

16. **Fear of castration.**   Some delusionally jealous persons fear that their partner will emasculate them.   They believe that their partner is trying to make them impotent or weaken them sexually.   Sometime, they suspect that their partner has given them "something" in their medicine or food to achieve that goal.   Partly, this problem is compounded by the fact that a person with insane jealousy is often impotent.   A delusionally jealous person comes to reason that impotence was brought about by their partner.

17. **Pseudomemory--false memory and recalls.**   The delusion of infidelity is so firmly entrenched in their mind, that in some cases, it also contaminates their memory.   A delusionally jealous person then begins to "recall" that, "Several men came to the house last night.   She thinks I don't know what she was doing with them," he complains bitterly.   Members of family vouch that no visitors came to the house that night but he remembers they did.

18. **Hallucinations.**   In cases of severely disabling mental illness, such as schizophrenia or psychotic mood disorder, a person may hear or see things that are really not there.   This can also happen, although not frequently, in a person with a jealous type delusional disorder, that is, where there is no other major psychiatric, organic, or chemical disorder, other than the delusional disorder of jealousy.   A person with jealous type delusional disorder may "see" tracks on the drive way or footprints in the yard which no other person sees; but that serves as an evidence that men have been coming to the house.   He may "hear" them talking to his partner or talking about his partner.

19. **Serious violence and assaultive behavior.**   Occasional violence and assaultive behavior is common in delusional jealousy.   But in some cases, there may be frequent and serious violence towards self or others.   I stress in some cases, not all, a person may become severely violent towards the partner or make a suicidal attempt.   Assaults on a rival or suspected rival are rare.   Reason for that may be that the rival is imaginary without a definite personal identity.   For the delusionally jealous male, rivals are "those men" and for the delusionally jealous female, they are "those women." But the compelling need to obtain confessions may lead to

physical assaults on the partner. Assaults may also occur during the jealous rage over their partner's ensuing "misdemeanors" and "transgressions."

These episodes of hitting and physical punishment may take place in the night in the privacy of their bedroom and even members of their family may not come to know about the violent episodes. A delusionally jealous man, in comparison to a delusionally jealous woman, is more likely to inflict injury to her female organs, an aggressive act, inflicted, out of jealous rage. He may also assault her for justified vengeance. He rarely feels remorseful for the acts of violence. A woman reported that her husband would repeatedly say, "Why don't you kill yourself and make us all happy?" However, in extreme cases, delusionally jealous persons kill themselves to put an end to their shame and pain, or they kill the spouse or the suspected rival out of hateful anger. If persecutory delusions are combined with the delusion of infidelity, be particularly watchful for any suicidal or homicidal behavior. For further discussion, refer to the section on "Insane Jealousy And Violence."

20. **Other delusions.** In some cases, other delusions, such as the delusion of persecution, of grandeur, or of influence may accompany the delusion of infidelity. Some persons with a delusional disorder may have more than one type of delusion. In major psychotic illness, there may be hallucinations and other delusions beside the delusion of infidelity. Sometimes, the delusion of infidelity may be the first one to show up before other psychotic symptoms become manifest.

In summary, a delusion of infidelity is born of sexual jealousy. A person comes to form an absolute conviction of the spouse's sexual misconduct without due cause. Delusionally jealous persons put in unrelenting efforts to provide proof of unfaithfulness in their partners. They want to know word by word what their partner said to their friends or relatives. They misinterpret trivial events and everyday occurrences. They see special meaning and foul play in their partner's chance encounters with other men in the street, untidiness of room, change of order, or of arrangement of articles in the house. They see a sexual motive and a sexual communication in the spouse's awkward and unintentional gesture, a slip of tongue, a facial grimace, and the like. They hunt for a sexual motive where there is none.

They may have sexual perversions and perform them on the spouse under the rationalization it satisfies her. They seem to derive pleasure from fantasizing the details of their partner's sexual encounters with other men. Some derive voyeuristic (Peeping Tom behavior) pleasure from secretively watching their partner in cleaning her private parts or engaged in biological functions. Although a delusionally jealous person abhors the thought of his partner even talking to another man, he may himself have engaged in a single or multiple extramarital relations.

They imagine and see vivid scenes of their spouse engaged in sexual indulgence. They may develop physical symptoms especially in the sex organs.

The desire to obtain proof is overwhelming. They make repeated attempts to force confession from the spouse. However, a false confession given by the spouse to pacify the delusionally jealous may prove to be futile.

In delusional jealousy, the basis of jealousy is false and untenable. However, the delusionally jealous person cannot be made to see that his accusations are false and baseless. He sticks to his delusion and goes on building on it arbitrarily without rules or logic. Innocent and inculpable behaviors of the partner are taken by him as renewed confirmation of his belief. Everyday events are interpreted as the evidence of sexual misconduct. A person has no way of avoiding these behaviors and situations which are misinterpreted by the jealous partner. Therefore a nonjealous partner has no way of not providing the delusionally jealous person further basis for new evidence and new accusations. All attempts to disprove his allegations are doomed to failure. He persists in his delusional ideas with renewed vigor and force.

A delusional person would not be willing to go to the clinic or the hospital for treatment. "There is nothing wrong with me," he would say. He would not want her to go to the clinic or a hospital because he is afraid she might get the opportunity to commit further sexual indiscretions. He may be afraid that she would go and tell someone about him and make him look bad. Also, agreeing to treatment would amount to an admission on his part that the fault lies in his own mind.

MORBID JEALOUSY AND DELUSIONAL JEALOUSY

SUMMARY OF COMPARISONS

All said and done, from a cursory look it is difficult to tell the difference between morbid jealousy and delusional jealousy. From outside appearance, these two look just the same. However, the difference really boils down to one thing, and that is the delusion of infidelity. If there is a delusion of infidelity, it is a delusional jealousy.

A delusionally jealous and a morbidly jealous person, both accuse the partner of infidelity. The difference is, how does each one arrive at the conclusion that his partner is unfaithful. For a morbidly jealous person, an outside observer, could still appreciate a chance of unfortunate misunderstanding; his doubt may be considered not too unreasonable a doubt. In the case of a delusionally jealous person, the doubt is clearly unreasonable. One can easily see the irrational nature of such thinking. There is no way any reasonable person can "jump" to that conclusion; it is not just a misinterpretation; it is a gross misinterpretation. For example, a morbidly jealous person overheard his wife on the phone talking to a friend, saying, "eight or ten." He jumped to the conclusion that she is pregnant by another man and her pregnancy is eight or ten weeks old. On the other hand, a delusionally jealous person does not need any suggestive words to draw such a conclusion. He may just see her talking on the phone, or standing in a particular position and he can be absolutely certain in his mind that she is pregnant by the man "she is fooling with."

A person with morbid jealousy may at times admit, "I may be wrong. There is not enough evidence for my suspicion." He may accept that there are some loopholes in his convictions. He cannot explain away all the facts and arguments presented by others to counter his reasoning but a delusionally jealous person does that in stride. A delusional person does not entertain any doubts whatsoever about the validity of his or her beliefs. Morbid jealousy has some flexibility of thinking while delusional jealousy has none.

Presence or absence of remorse is an important criteria in differentiating the two. A morbidly jealous person, in his better moments, feels remorseful, tenders an apology, and even tries to make up to his partner for his regretful behavior. He may bring expensive gifts to make up for his irrational behavior and cry and beg to be forgiven. In fact, he may go into cycles of rage and remorse. But a delusionally jealous person feels "justified" for all the pain and violence, he extends to the partner. Furthermore, an apology is only possible if a person feels he was wrong or got carried away; a delusionally jealous person does not entertain any doubts about his fixed beliefs.

In summary, answers to the following questions will help you to determine whether you are dealing with morbid jealousy or delusional jealousy. Positive answers to two or more of the following indicate delusional jealousy:

1. Is the reasoning for arriving at the conclusion delusional? What are the facts and the bases of the evidence?
2. Are there gross misperceptions and misinterpretations?
3. Is there a lack of remorse for violence towards the partner in a person who can feel remorse and guilt for his actions towards others?
4. Is there a sense of desperation in obtaining a confession from the partner?
5. Is there a pseudomemory related to the "unfaithful behavior" and related events?

6.   Are there hallucinations related to the "unfaithful behavior" and related events?

7. Is there a delusion concerning the partner poisoning the jealous partner, having venereal disease, horrible infection, etc.?

DELUSIONAL DISORDER OF JEALOUSY

The delusion of infidelity, in some cases, may be a by-product of some other severe mental disorder.   In other words, a severe mental disorder, such as schizophrenia, manic-depressive disorder, or psychotic depression may be a primary disorder and delusional jealousy may be secondary to it.   However, delusional disorder of jealousy is a free standing mental disorder. It means that delusional jealousy is not a part of some other mental disorder. It is a disorder by itself. There is no other significant problem except that of delusional jealousy. Make no mistakes about it; it is a very serious problem by itself. This is the most deceptive form of disorder. The person with this disorder manifests a delusion of infidelity but does not have any other mental disorder which may be responsible for his delusion.

As discussed earlier, psychotic mental disorders, such as schizophrenia, manic-depressive, psychotic depression, are not the only conditions which can produce delusional jealousy. Physical, chemical, and organic disorders can also cause delusional jealousy. And so can certain kinds of brain disorders or brain abnormalities. For instance, some people with temporal epilepsy, or Huntington's Chorea may have delusions. Certain lesions in the brain, particularly in the right hemisphere, are known to cause delusions. Certain chemical substances, such as cocaine can also present a picture similar to a delusional disorder. Also, amphetamines, cannabis, cocaine, PCP, and hallucinogens can cause delusions.   Only when the delusion of infidelity seems to have been caused by nonorganic factors, can a diagnosis of delusional disorder of jealousy be given.

Temporal epilepsy, brain lesions, dementia, brain damage, and the like, can be diagnosed from the events in the individual's history, such as accidents and head injuries, and from medical laboratory examinations.

In brief, major guidelines and diagnostic criteria for the delusional disorder of jealousy are as follows:

1. Delusion of infidelity.
2. No psychotic mental disorder.
3. No history of and not caused by chronic and severe abuse of chemicals such as alcohol, cocaine, amphetamines, etc.
4. No disorder of mood such as the presence of a depressed or the elated mood.
5. Absence of an organic disorder, such as epilepsy, brain damage, stroke, dementia, etc.

A person with delusional disorder of jealousy may be unimpaired in his functions in other life areas. He may be a hard working, conscientious, and earnest worker. He may come across as a normal social person to outsiders. He may not have had any clash with law and order. He may be generally affectionate to his children (provided he is sure of the paternity). His reasoning and logical thinking may be intact in all other areas. In fact, he is "normal" in all other areas except in his relationship with his partner. Only his spouse and children may know about his problem, and in some cases, spouses have hidden it from their children too. Since he is so normal in all other areas, the victim-partner does not suspect the presence of a mental disorder. In the worst scenario, victim-partners blame themselves and go on a guilt trip.

BEHAVIORAL EXAMPLES OF INSANE JEALOUSY

We have made an effort to give concrete behavioral examples of the "signs" of insane jealousy or delusional jealousy described earlier, wherever it was possible. However, the signs also include descriptions which are not observable from the outside by another person. In this section we have chosen examples from actual case histories, of behaviors which can be observed by another person directly without making any assumptions or inferences. These behavioral examples of insane jealousy may be broadly classified in three groups: **Misperceptions and misinterpretations** of everyday actions and trivia; **Domestic espionage; and Controls and restrictions.** Examples under each group will be of interest in recognizing the concrete signs of insane jealousy.

MISPERCEPTIONS AND MISINTERPRETATIONS

1. If a car passes slowly by his house, he accuses her that her lover is waiting for him to get out of the house so that he can get in with her.

2. If a driver in a passing by car turns on his headlight, he argues with his partner that the driver is giving a secret signal for her.

3. If he sees a stain on the carpet or on the bedclothes, rearrangement of the furniture in the house, or a hair in the bed or on the clothes, he accuses her of infidelity.

4. If she sits sideways on the chair, stands a little awkwardly, or looks restless, he questions what she has done and who she has been with.

5. When someone on the other end of the telephone says, "Wrong number," and hangs up, he questions his partner about who it was and why he is calling at home.

6. If she has used perfume, he accuses her of trying to take away the body smell of her lover or "freshening up" after the misdeed.

7. If she comes home late from work, he accuses her of meeting her lover.

8. If she touches her hair or face, moves her eyes, and makes any body movements in the presence of other men, he complains that she was making sexual gestures and was signing them to "come on."

9. When a wrinkle is noticed on the bedsheet, the make-up or the lipstick looks thin, clothes look crumpled, a button is unbuttoned, and the like, he accuses her of unfaithful acts.

CONTROLS AND RESTRICTIONS

1. Does not allow her to go out into the yard.
2. Does not allow her to answer the telephone.
3. Does not allow her to answer the door.
4. Does not allow her to go out to meet friends, not even close relatives.
5. Goes into a rage and flurry of accusations if his partner ran into a friend or an acquaintance and came later than usual.
6. Does not allow his partner to do anything on her own unless it is absolutely unavoidable. He would wait for her for hours if he has to, but take her everywhere she needs to go.
7. Objects to her going to work, if she is employed.
8. He must pick her places of employment. He may reject a place of work because there are "too many men." He would insist that the workers must be all women. If she must go to work for other compelling reasons, he would insist to drop her off and pick her up personally.
9. Does not allow her in the first place, or goes into a rage afterwards, if his partner talks to people of opposite sex in a social gathering or public place.

DOMESTIC ESPIONAGE

1. Searching partner's pockets and clothes, especially, the underwear, for evidence of unfaithfulness. Checking the pocketbook for addresses and telephone numbers.
2. Listening in on phone conversations.
3. Examining receipts and bills to look for unaccounted expenses. Keeping close tabs on the bank account, pay stubs, and all earnings.
4. Reading partner's mail surreptitiously.
5. Hiring private detectives to spy on the partner.
6. Following the partner to work, surreptitiously, from a distance.
7. Makes unannounced, surprise visits or telephone calls at partner's work place to check, or visits the carparking lot to confirm the presence of her car.
8. Pantychecks. Examining the underclothings, such as the undies, panties and brassieres for evidence of sexual

misconduct, especially if the partner or he himself has been away from the house.

9. Examining the bathroom, bedroom, and other places of the house with meticulous care for misconduct during the unsupervised time.

10. Examining the phone bills for any unauthorized calls.

11. Checking the trashcan for cancelled notes and any other possible incriminating documents.

12. Listening to family conversations while under the pretense of sleeping.

13. Using binoculars to spy on his partner from afar.

14. After pretending to leave the house, reentering surreptitiously in an attempt to verify the incidence of unfaithfulness.

15. Asking probing questions to children for possible clues of his partner's sexual misconduct.

16. Investigating the potential lover, his whereabouts, and absences for tallying with the partner's movements.

17. Body check. Checking partner's body for tell tale signs of sexual misbehavior.

18. Keeping a secret record of the mileage on the odometer of the partner's car. Comparing it every day with the mileage supposed to be travelled by the partner.

19. Measuring the time taken to travel from one place to another. Comparing it with the time taken by the partner to a particular place as claimed by her.

JEALOUSY BEHAVIORS

Some behaviors indicate that he is jealous of the partner herself. He experiences direct feelings of jealousy towards the partner; he is either competing with her or resents her attractiveness, intelligence or other enviable qualities. Here are some examples of the jealousy behaviors towards the partner:

1. He does not let her shave her legs, use bright lipsticks, or wear make up because that makes her "too attractive for men."

2. He ruins or cuts her dress into shreds because it looks "too good" on her.

3. If someone pays a compliment to his partner he gets real upset and later on quarrels with his partner, either for dressing up too much, or paying too much attention to the person who paid compliments.

4. He complains that everyone talks to her and comes to see her only; no one is there for him.

5. He compares the presents, greetings, hugs and the similar tokens of affection, given to her and him, and complains that "they all are on her side and no one cares about him."

6. He displays his unhappiness and anger with people (even his children), who express love and affection to his partner or pay more attention to her.

7. He resents her attractiveness, beauty, and other personal, social qualities and taunts her about them in a sarcastic or put-down manner. He would often point out "how stupid and dumb" the partner is and tell her, "Nobody can like you," or "You can never do anything right."

INSANELY JEALOUS: PERSONAL CHARACTERISTICS

Insane jealousy can develop in a person who has shown particular psychological- emotional characteristics in the past or is displaying them at present. These characteristics indicate a potential for insane jealousy. They suggest that a person is predisposed to develop insane jealousy and under the right circumstances, given certain key experiences, he may succumb to insane jealousy. Some of the qualities and attributes listed here are opposite of each other and may exclude one another. This contradiction is understandable as insane jealousy does not afflict just one type of person; it can overcome personalities which are very different from one another. The psychological-emotional characteristics that precede or accompany insane jealousy are described below. Several of these may be present in a given case:

1. Lacks trust in one's own self. A person who constantly tells himself, "I am no good. I am not lovable."

2. Lacks trust in others. A person who possesses attitudes of distrust and suspicion towards others; that is, one who shows paranoid trends. Such a person is constantly repeating in his mind statements to the effect of, "It is a dog eat dog world. No body cares about another. No body gives a damn. They do not love me. They will hurt me. I had better watch out."

3. Very possessive.

4. Tends to get easily frustrated and dissatisfied with life.

5. Quick tempered. If he was violent in his childhood, he is likely to be violent with his partner during his jealous rages.

6. Egotistic, self-centered, conceited, and selfish. Such a person is also imposing and opinionated.

7. Aggressive, daring, hostile person who has a problem with anger.

8. The macho type, who has very traditional, conservative, ideas and attitudes regarding men and women. Such men are likely to call their partner, "doll," "honey," "baby," "girl" and the like. However, when in a jealous rage, their most favorite word is, "whore" and the second favorite, "slut," using the latter in the sense of a woman of loose character.

9. Has a low self-esteem. Lacks confidence and feeling of personal efficacy.

10. Has few friends. If he makes friends, he cannot keep the friendship for long. Has difficulty in establishing close friendships. Lack of close friends could be observed in childhood in relation to other peers of his age. He is described by some as "aloof" or "solitary."

11. Afraid of intimacy. In adolescence and adulthood, fear of intimacy may be apparent to someone who tries to be close to them. Intimacy makes them feel vulnerable. They may be described as "wary" by people who formed some sort of friendship with them.

12. Unable to love. Unable to genuinely nurture others. It is said that a person who becomes insanely jealous is basically unable to love anyone. Other relationships may lack feelings and open communication.

13. Has a problem with latent or suppressed homosexuality. Overtly, he may have a strong hatred for homosexuals which is one way of fighting with the homosexual attraction and impulses. His macho demeanor is another indication of homosexual impulses. He has a tendency to fantasize about

persons of the same sex engaged in sexual activity with his partner. It provides him sexual pleasure. Some people go to the extent of asking or forcing their partner to have sex with a person of their own sex. This is one of the most puzzling behavior of insane jealousy and has led many psychologists to speculate that jealousy is basically an inverted homosexuality. It means that an insanely jealous person is seeking a sexual partner of his own sex through the opposite-sex partner.

14. Has poor social skills. Incidentally, lack of social skills and qualities may directly cause him to feel inferior to others in general and in specific to the partner.

15. Dependent on others. When he comes to live with his partner, all his needs are to be met by the partner. It is like he has a "mother fixation" on her. He wants his partner to almost bathe him, clothe him, feed him, carry everything to him as he wants it. He desperately clutches to the partner, as if saying, "Now I have got you. I will never let you go."

16. Sensitive and touchy. Sometimes, it is described as "irritable sensitivity."

17. Shy and unassertive. This trait is easily observed by others and reported by the individual himself if questions are asked about his school days in relation to other peers.

18. Feels very insecure. There may be a generalized life-long feeling of insecurity that he has carried with himself.

19. Depressive and pessimistic. Takes the worst possible view of people and the world, and draws the worst scenario in his mind.

20. Narcissistic. Spouses of jealous partners have reported that their jealous partners would stand in front of the mirror for long periods of time admiring themselves; they work hard to look just right. Jealousy disordered persons are in love with themselves and easily threatened by others. Overtly they may act superior, but just below the skin, they feel inferior to everybody around.

21. Masochistic (self-punishing and self-defeating) tendencies and behavior. This can be inferred from childhood memories of some insanely jealous persons who used to see themselves punished and hurt. In adulthood, they have such fantasies as their partner making fun of them to others, the partner and the rival conspiring to hurt and

humiliate them, or making love with each other and having fun when the jealous partner is lying on the death bed.

22. In the case of a male, basically a "misogynist," having hatred for the entire female class. This hatred and suspicion extends even to one's own sisters and daughters because they belong to female genre.

23. Has a very unrealistic image of an ideal lover. He never reconciles or adjusts to a real person in life. As a result he has too unrealistic expectations which cannot be met through his relationship with his partner. He becomes frustrated, critical, and jealous of his partner.

24. Tends to have stormy and impulsive relationships. He falls headlong in love. He and his partner may label it as a "romantic relationship." But the seeds of jealousy may be apparent even in the dating behavior.

25. Intensely jealous. He may be jealous of practically everyone around, men or women. In childhood, he may have shown intense jealousy in relation to his siblings.

26. Rigid and stubborn.

27. Obsessive-compulsive. He may show strong need for order and methodical approach. He may be particular about the small details of how something needs to be done or arranged. For example, clothes have to be arranged in a certain order in the closet, or door locks and electrical plugs have to be checked, several times a day. He may be a perfectionist. These characteristics indicate anxiety and an enormous need to exercise control.

28. Odd, eccentric, cynical.

29. Carries a general sense of failure about life and about himself. "No matter what I do it is not enough. Nothing comes out right."

30. Superficially gregarious and socially overactive. However, in intimate relationships, all his feelings of insecurity and jealousy come out from under. Such a person presents one example of the Jekyll and Hyde-type person that we discussed earlier.

31. Emotionally immature personality.

32. Tends to ruminate obsessively. His thoughts may have an obsessional quality. A thought may come to his mind over and over again, and in spite of his trying, he can't get the thought out of his mind. Therefore, when jealousy sets in, his thoughts about his partner and the rival assume an

obsessional character. Then he ruminates about the acts of unfaithfulness, "Where did she go? What did she say she was going to do?"

The following descriptions of jealousy disordered husbands were given by women in our group discussion:

My husband was a con artist. If he couldn't convince you, he would go an extra ten miles to convince you. He would manipulate you to prove himself right. He has to be right all the time. I as a woman could never be right.

This kind of person never leaves you alone. Once they got you, they are always after you. They think their family is perfect and yours is low class.

In the beginning of our marriage, he held it together, he put up an act, then it fell apart and he came out with his strange thoughts.

When he was away from home, he would phone me all the time. If kids said, "Mom is in the bathroom," he would immediately get paranoid, "Why is she in the bathroom?"

I knew something was wrong, but I was terrified to ask. Someone you love, you want to find excuses for them. My self-esteem was too low, how could I say something was wrong with him and not with me? He would draw you in to his sickness. He would make you feel it's your fault.

They are women haters. They are contemptuous of women as a whole. They castigate all women as one. When they are angry, it comes out as, "whore" or "slut." They would be vicious to you and then wouldn't remember it at all or act as if nothing happened. If they want to apologize to you they can do it so well that it would tear your heart apart.

They have double standards, one for themselves, and one for you. When you simply talk to a man, you are flirting. When you catch them with their pants down with another woman, they say, "It's not my fault. She kept coming at me."

They want you to wear clothes to cover up as if they are ashamed of you.

They have to physically hurt you in order to sexually perform and stimulate themselves. They call you "nympho" so you cut off your body. When you are beaten and degraded then they want to make love to you.

Jealous men can't tolerate anybody cutting them on the road. If somebody does, they will chase them. They have to be in complete control of every situation.

HIDDEN GAINS OF INSANE JEALOUSY

Insane jealousy, like many other emotional disorders, is not without "secondary gains." By secondary gains, psychologists mean that a problem, of course, hurts but it also pays. Some people find jealousy flattering (at least in the beginning), they feel valued and loved; if their partners don't let them get out of their sight and don't let them talk to anyone, they feel "special." Some partners may, without being aware of it, provoke jealousy. They remain characteristically mysterious and vague in their answers when questioned by the jealous partner as they secretly enjoy the partner being jealous. Some nonjealous partners soon realize the power they have over their partners, how easily they can get under the skin of nonjealous partners, by flirting a little, or being sought out by others.

These are risky games and the cost may be far too much for the gains made. However, the fact is that there may be some obvious and not so obvious gains to one or both partners accruing from jealousy. These may not be engineered by either partner and they may not be consciously exploited by either partner. Such gains are listed below:

Due to insane jealousy, both partners, for different reasons, may try to improve on their image and make themselves more attractive and try to be more competitive.

Insane jealousy may reduce the pain of feeling worthless and inferior or whatever negative emotion one may be suffering from. A jealous partner doesn't have to look for such negative feelings in his own self; he can hold his partner responsible for his feeling worthless and hopeless. At the same time, the nonjealous partner can feel worthy and valued.

Insane jealousy may bring some excitement in a marriage that is going dull or where the partners may be drifting apart for unacknowledged reasons.

The insanely jealous feels that he is being very patient with his partner and putting up with all the humiliation and hurt of her indiscriminate behavior, and he is therefore entitled to compensation. To some extent, it does work. The accused partner tries to do everything to comfort him, please him, and not do anything that upsets him.

Jealousy increases the sexual desire. The threatened loss of partner stimulates his interest to make him more competitive. In some cases, the "visions" of what his partner and the supposed rival might be doing together, may sexually excite him. Actually some insanely jealous persons become hypersexual, which in their mind, is absolutely essential to save the marriage. They reason that an extraordinary amount of sexual activity may prevent her from sexual misbehaviors with other men. Some take that as a cause to initiate their own unfulfilled sexual perversions on their partner to satisfy her lust and "kinky" desires.

The flip side of the above mentioned coin is that many jealous partners are impotent. They hold their partner's sexual misconduct responsible for killing their sexual desire. By this rationalization, they do not have to admit to themselves that they indeed have become impotent, and if they do someone else is responsible for their impotence, not they.

Insane jealousy can also give expression to one's suppressed or unfulfilled homosexual desires and impulses. It is known from the clinical reports of the treatment of some insanely jealous persons that they have dreams or masturbatory phantasies in which they see themselves engaged in sexual activities with a person of same sex. An insanely jealous person may also fantasize that he and another man or men are engaged in sexual activity together with his partner. At times an insanely jealous person, during foreplay or actual intercourse may have fantasies about the rival or may imagine that he is transformed into a rival. Some insanely jealous men can only reach an orgasm by watching their partner in intercourse with another man. In some cases, there appears to be a preoccupation, on the part of the insanely jealous, with the person and especially the body of the rival. Some report experiencing sexual excitement in fantasizing about the naked body of the rival and his private parts, suggesting that the insanely jealous derives some homosexual pleasure from such fantasies.

Resolution of guilt resulting from one's own unfaithfulness. He is projecting his own unfaithfulness on to the partner. By imagining that his partner is unfaithful, he does not have to feel guilty anymore for his unfaithfulness.

Insane jealousy helps to compensate for the feelings of inferiority to one's partner. The jealous partner can then feel morally superior.

Insane jealousy provides a justification as well as the outlet for feelings of anger, hate, envy, and other similar unresolved negative feelings that a jealous partner experiences towards the partner and significant others.

He projects his own sexual fantasies onto the partner and sees her acting on all those forbidden impulses and desires, the things that he wished he could do.

FAMILY AND PERSONAL BACKGROUND OF AN INSANELY JEALOUS PERSON

Father or mother may be intensely jealous. A parent may teach him to distrust and suspect all outsiders. It may be a very closed family system which views people from outside as untrustworthy. In such a family, the partner of a would-be insanely jealous person is seen as an outsider and an object of suspicion. His parents may collaborate with him in developing a paranoid and distrustful relationship towards the victim partner. An insanely jealous person, in such a case, may solicit help from parent or parents to keep a watch on the partner. In cases, where a parent is also insanely jealous, they together may share some delusions against the suspected spouse.

He may have experienced a sexual trauma in early years. For example, he may have witnessed mother being promiscuous and unfaithful. Her indulgence with different men may have caused her to neglect him in his childhood.

History of sexual and or physical abuse in childhood and or adolescence.

Large families with the presence of multiple siblings. However, their birth order does not make a difference; the insanely jealous could be the oldest, middle, or younger. I have not come across an insanely jealous person who was the only child of his parents. It is speculated that a large family in some way contributes to the formation of abnormal jealousy.

He may be extremely attached and loyal to his parents. However, in some cases, he may have enormous hostility against one or both parents. Such hostility is seen in cases where there is a history of trauma, abuse, or neglect at the hands of parents.

WHAT TRIGGERS INSANE JEALOUSY

Insane jealousy may not be evident from day one of the marriage. Sometime it may take a long time, even years, and then one day it hits abruptly, and with shocking intensity. In such cases, insane jealousy is there, it is buried deep and one day it all comes out.

Insane jealousy is "episodic" or "phasic" which means that it comes in phases. It may appear at some point of time with full intensity and strength and dominate the entire thinking and feeling world of a person, then disappear--only to surface later with equal intensity and force.

So what triggers insane jealousy or what intensifies it so that an individual, at certain points, is unable to contain it within himself?

The insanely jealous persons may tell you that the first thing they noticed which made them suspicious was a change in their partner's feelings towards them: "She seemed to turn against me, acted real cold,"; "She lost all interest in me, I didn't know what was going on,"; "She didn't like anymore what I said or did or what I stood for." However, these may well be the projections of the insanely jealous persons on their partners. In reality it is they, who out of their insane jealousy, develop so much disaffection for their partners that they lose all interest and turn cold towards them.

It is probable that victim-partners, over a period of time, unrequited and rebuffed for their love may become emotionally distant and withdrawn from their insanely jealous partners. On the other hand, some victim-partners report that they thought everything was going great and wonderful in marriage and then one day their partner started questioning them about the phone calls and letters from their relatives and of their opposite-sex friends before marriage. These victims report that the questioning by their partner was so direct and insistent, their anger so vicious and their language so foul that they were shocked by the suddenness and intensity of it. It seems that an insanely jealous person might have been brooding and ruminating over his thoughts that, "She has really changed and she doesn't love me anymore," or "She was and is a whore and I am beginning to find out now." Then he would start looking at everything with that mind set and find evidence in everyday events and occurrences.

Following is a list of factors that have been associated with either the triggering off or the intensification of insane jealousy:

1. **His extra-marital affair**. Abnormal jealousy may appear on the scene after a brief or prolonged incidence of infidelity on the part of the insanely jealous person. Some men are reported to have been promiscuous prior to the onset of insane jealousy. This type of jealousy is referred to as the "projective jealousy," that is, a situation, in which

promiscuous persons are projecting their unacceptable infidelity onto their partners.

2. **Her extra-marital affair.** Another triggering factor for appearance of pathologic jealousy may be a discovery or disclosure of infidelity on the part of the victim-partner. Insane jealousy may set off immediately after the partner finds out about the infidelity or it may start as a jealousy after the discovery of an extra-marital affair and gradually intensify to the degree of insane jealousy.

3. **Onset of impotence on the part of the male.** Impotence lowers his self-esteem and he begins to suspect that since he can't perform, she will seek sexual satisfaction elsewhere.

4. **Onset of her frigidity.** A female partner becomes sexually frigid or there occurs a reduction in her emotional or sexual response towards him. As a reaction to this change, he begins to suspect that her loss of interest in him is due to her sexual adventures outside their relationship.

5. **Marital problems and tension.** Instead of dealing with the actual source of tension, one partner becomes insanely jealous. Some who develop impotence with the jealousy seem to be able to perform sexually only after a major fight. They need a fight and a sexual make-up for temporary escapades from jealousy.

6. **Injury, accident, or a disabling illness.** Persons with a potential for insane jealousy may manifest problems when they receive serious injury, develop a major illness, or are involved in a serious accident. Such conditions may involve prolonged dependence, cause disability and damage their self-esteem, which may contribute to the emergence of insane jealousy.

7. **Continued and prolonged levels of severe stress.** Preoccupation and ruminations with jealousy divert the focus from the problem.

8. **Alcoholism.** Long-term and heavy use of alcohol impairs personal, social, and occupational performance. It causes isolation, guilt, depression, impotence and many other negative consequences. An alcoholic person begins to suspect that his partner is abandoning him in favor of others. There is a special name for this product, which is "alcoholic jealousy."

9. **Substance abuse**. Substances, such as cocaine, PCP, and marijuana, may cause a paranoid state in which a person feels persecuted by others or betrayed by his own partner.

10. **Onset of a mental disorder**. Insane jealousy may also emerge when one of the partners develops a mental disorder. Such a mental disorder could belong to a neurotic or a psychotic type of illness. Amongst the neurotic disorders, severe and generalized anxiety disorders, phobias (irrational and exaggerated fears), obsessive-compulsive disorders (persistent unwelcome thoughts and compulsive behavior) and hypochondriasis (imaginary illness), are specially noted for accompanying insane jealousy.

Insane jealousy may sometimes appear as the first sign of a psychotic illness. In some cases, schizophrenia and manic-depressive disorders, particularly with paranoid features, initially manifest themselves as symptoms of insane jealousy. In such cases the content of the delusions and hallucinations, at least in the beginning, may be primarily, the supposed unfaithfulness of the partner.

11. **Organic damage.** Brain damage, strokes, brain lesions, and other neurological diseases that affect the central nervous system may be followed by insane jealousy as the person becomes deeply aware of his deficiencies and develops inferiority and insecurity. Patients of dementia, Parkinson's disease, epilepsy, Huntington's chorea, pituitary dysfunction, have been brought to the clinics with problems of insane jealousy. Careful medical investigations in these cases identified neurological disorders which contributed to the problems of insane jealousy.

12. **Onset of pregnancy** or childbirth. A man may suspect that his partner has conceived the baby in an illicit union with another man and consequently develop insane jealousy. Jealousy disordered men, when they come to know that their partner is pregnant, are frequently reported to fly in to a rage, and kick her or hurt her in the tummy where the baby is. They are suspicious that someone else is the father. They are jealous of the baby and they compete with the baby for the breast milk; they want to nurse the milk. In the case of jealousy disordered females, a woman, during pregnancy or after, may become insanely jealous if she feels that she is no more sexually attractive to her partner, or she suspects

that while she is tied down with the baby at home, he is running around with other women.

13. **Feelings of decline and loss.** The sense of loss in women may be related to menopause, or to middle age disillusionment and disappointment in both men and women. Some people have referred to it as "middle age impotence."

14. **Depression.** Depression is frequently associated with insane jealousy. Many times, depression may be the primary problem and jealousy secondary to this emotional disturbance. When a person feels depressed, he feels inferior and insecure. He imagines the worst of himself and of others. He may feel that no body likes him and even his partner has deserted him in favor of others. However, it is not always easy to tell if depression caused jealousy or jealousy caused depression.

15. **Onset of old age.** Insane jealousy can appear in old age when a couple is struck with an empty nest. They may retire from an active engagement and pursuit of interests. They may become socially isolated. Some may resent the sags around their eyes, the greying of the hair, the deepening wrinkles, and the loosely hanging skin. At any rate, many insanely jealous persons come to the attention of outside agencies in their middle age years. It could be that the sense of loss in middle age triggered off the jealousy or that the culmination of the jealousy for years became so unbearable that the couple asked for · professional intervention. In some cases, the grown up children are instrumental in bringing their troubled parents to the clinic.

16. **"January and May" syndrome.** Jealousy may be triggered in a case in which an old man marries a young woman or vice versa. In the "Merchant's Tale," one of the tales composed by Chaucer in the famous Canterbury Tales, January is the old man and May is the young lady. January is depicted as the old, insecure, and jealous man. According to this syndrome, an old man who marries a young woman becomes insanely jealous and is obsessed with the thoughts of her forsaking him and with the fears of the rivals decamping with her.

17. **Sensory impairment such as blindness or deafness.** The sensory loss not only generates the feelings of general loss, inferiority, and insecurity but he may also "see" or

"hear" things according to his worst fears uncorrected by his failing senses.

18. **Psychosocial changes.** Psychosocial changes such as the migration, displacement, loss of employment, relocation, natural disasters, and other forms of personal-social crises are also known to trigger off insane jealousy. All such events can produce a sense of alienation, hopelessness, and lack of confidence.

19. **Loss of a parent.** Loss of a parent may be a significant factor in case of a partner who is still emotionally or psychologically dependent on his or her parent. Death of parent to whom one was strongly emotionally bonded can cause abnormal levels of anxiety and insecurity. The grieving person may transfer massive emotional needs and expectations onto one's partner, get easily frustrated and become insanely jealous.

20. **Distorted communication between the partners.** A partner may provoke jealousy by not giving a straight answer in the hope of generating passionate love. With innuendoes and vague allusions, a partner may unwittingly plant suspicions in the mind of the jealousy prone partner. Due to this half-concealment, mystery, and suspense, a couple may have to pay the cost in the form of insane jealousy.

21. **Development of a sense of inferiority in relation to one's partner.** A partner, in the course of marriage, may make extraordinary strides in career, social status, and other avenues of achievement. The other partner, may feel socially inferior and or develop feelings of competition and rivalry towards the felt superior partner. The partner who feels inferior may feel jealous of the qualities and attributes of the other and develop sexual jealousy.

22. **Revival of feelings of deprivation.** The need to be loved increases to an extraordinary degree due to childhood emotional deprivation or loss of love. The stronger the need for love, the greater the chances of experiencing jealousy. The person who needs extraordinary love, may keep a constant vigil on the partner lest she becomes disloyal. The need for love may reach desperation in a person who is basically dependent and emotionally immature.

23. **Identification with the rival.** An insanely jealous person may unconsciously identify with a rival, "He reminds

me of myself. I think she loves in him what I was or what I
could have been."

24.   **Arousal of homosexual attraction towards a
suspected rival.** Arousal of subconcious or conscious
homosexual interest in the rival or opposite sex in general
may contribute to the development of a pathologic jealousy.
A jealousy prone person may develop sexual fantasies about
the rival either directly engaged in sexual activity with him
or with the accused. As these fantasies provide sexual
gratification, they become more frequent. Jealousy makes a
person brood and ruminate, see in his mind over and again,
the vivid sexual acts that the partner and the rival may be
engaging in. It is true that jealousy is pain, but as one can
see, it also provides sexual pleasure. Gradually, insane
jealousy gets firmly rooted in the mind of a jealous partner.
See the section on the "Hidden Gains of Insane Jealousy."

25. **Experience of guilt in relation to one's partner.** A
person may feel guilty for his own unfaithful behavior. This
guilt may trigger off insane jealousy to assuage his feelings
of guilt because the other partner is indulging in worse acts.
Guilt may also be produced by sexual desires and impulses
towards others, whether he acted upon them or not. Such a
guilt may also be alleviated or replaced by "justified" anger
towards the partner for her supposedly unfaithful deeds.

INSANE JEALOUSY AND VIOLENCE

Society remains unaware of violence arising out of insane
jealousy. It is a seriously underreported human tragedy.

Insane jealousy is a potentially violent condition. One out
of twelve murders in the U.S.A. is committed by his or her
spouse. The number one motive in spousal homicide is
jealousy. According to the Canadian police, jealousy
accounts for one out of every five spousal homicides; a
highly significant fact in itself, but it does not tell the
complete story. Many homicides are simply identified as,
"domestic disputes," "argument," and "self-defense" which
really stem from sexual jealousy.

Reports indicate that anywhere between 20 to 85 per cent of spousal homicides are committed on account of sexual jealousy.

Male jealousy far surpasses female jealousy as a homicide motive. The ratio of violent jealous males to females is roughly four to one and in some studies even more. Men are definitely more violent in matters of sexual jealousy.

Most of the studies only take homicide into consideration. Serious jealousy-related physical injuries which fall short of murder are not taken into account. The number of violent attacks is much higher than that of murderous assaults but it is rarely reported. Spousal killing is not the only problem for a woman whose husband is sexually jealous. For every murdered wife, hundreds are punched, bruised and intimidated.

A large number of batterers are sexually jealous. Sexually jealous men seem to have enormous need for control over women and they don't settle for anything less than absolute control. Battering is often triggered by suspicions of infidelity. A batterer in a typical battering incident calls her a "whore," "broad," "cunt," or other similar names which indicate sexual jealousy. Many male batterers initiate battering when they come to know about the partner's pregnancy for the first time. Many a time, restrictions are placed on the partner, not so much to hide the battering, but mainly to prevent her from coming into contact with the threatening rivals, her friends, and relatives.

Many suicidal attempts and cases of successful suicide are committed by victim-partners and the insanely jealous; they are not likely to be reported as jealousy-driven acts.

"Trivial altercations," "domestic disputes," and "jealousy" are reported as the three largest motives of all incidents of homicide. It is our position that a very large number of the cases subsumed under these three categories pertain to insane jealousy. We invite researchers to investigate the validity of our assumption.

EVALUATION AND TREATMENT

Families are reluctant to see insane jealousy as a part of mental illness. Victim-spouses consider it as their fault or as an inevitable product of the marital relationship. Children of an insanely jealous person may not understand what is going on between the parents, until much later. A person with a jealousy disorder rarely sees it as his problem. In our experience, a few people, who tried to do something about the problem by involving outside people, didn't know how to go about it, who to contact and what would be relevant to tell. Specific education and awareness is required for the affected people and the professional community. In this section we intend to provide specific directions for counselors and families to enter into a joint endeavor to attack the problem. We also intend to provide ideas and directions for men and women, individually, and as couples, to help themselves and work towards further self-growth. A jealousy disorder is a very obstinate condition, please seek help immediately!

Insane jealousy can be the first symptom of a number of different psychiatric disorders before other symptoms become apparent. Consult a mental health professional, such as a psychiatrist or a psychologist, to diagnose the primary illness. If you have noticed any other strange or unusual behavior, do mention it to the professional.

STRUCTURE OF ASSESSMENT INTERVIEWS

A counselor must arrange for individual interviews with each partner, beside the joint interview.

A counselor must assess the dangerousness before sharing the "sensitive" material revealed by the nonjealous partner in the individual interviews.

If possible, a male and a female counselor should conduct the interviews together, especially, the individual interviews.

In situations, where there is a serious potential for violence, or husband and wife are estranged, the couple may be seen, preferably, in separate buildings, by different counselors, and if they have to be seen in the same building, they must be seen on different days, at different times. Also, the appointments have to be kept confidential, even from husband and wife. It should be stated as a policy at the time of the intake.

The nonjealous partner, especially, if it happens to be a woman, must be offered a support group. If no such support group and shelter is available in the community, counselors should encourage the local humanitarian agencies to form a support group and shelter for women.

Just as in a child abuse situation, so in violent jealousy, a victim-partner does need legal and physical protection. In the case of a violent and aggressive partner, a counselor, district attorney, and other social and legal agencies, need to get together to ask the court to order him or her to move out of the house unless significant progress is observed by the helping agencies. A counselor may coordinate this action with other agencies. In other situations, the victim herself, or other agencies in behalf of the victim, may approach the judge who may order the police for a temporary arrest and bring the jealousy disordered person to a clinic for mental evaluation. We hope that the counselor who is asked to do such an evaluation has read this book to enable him or her for an accurate assessment of the seriousness of the situation.

Counselors must claim the responsibility for determining the progress or lack thereof, based on their own **judgment** rather than the on the **information,** for example, "She told me you are still accusing her and arguing with her." That could be dangerous for the health of a victim-partner. A jealousy disordered person may be threatening her to not tell what is really going on. He may also get upset with her that she is not telling the counselor the right things to bring him back.

Counselors have to sometimes question the partners aggressively if it seems there is more to it than meets the eye. One woman, whose husband was delusionally jealous and violent, said, "When I went for therapy, I would expect that the doctor would see it through but my husband would con them. The doctor wouldn't see it through and then I would also act as if everything was okay."

Counselors need to explain the structure and purpose of the assessment at the very outset to cut down on the suspicion. A couple needs to be told that it is important for progress that each one can tell them what is going on without fearing negative consequences.

A clinician needs to determine if the jealousy disorder is with or without the delusion of infidelity. If you are a victim-partner, inform the clinician if your partner has ever admitted that he was wrong in making these accusations or promised you that he would not suspect you in this manner again. It is very important that you inform the counselor if your partner has accused you of doing something because he says, "I remember what you did," which you know you never did. Also, make a point to inform your counselor if your partner has expressed any other type of delusions, such as of being poisoned or persecuted in some other way. Inform the counselor if your partner is hearing or seeing things that are not really there.

A counselor must also determine the potential for danger, that is of suicide and homicide, and recommend hospitalization, temporary separation, or divorce, if necessary.

Include children in family therapy if the conflict also centers around your children.

Discuss the jealousy behavior in its totality, not just the sexual jealousy. Discuss the experience of jealousy in your childhood, in relation to your siblings, parents, and peers. Discuss present problems of jealousy in relation to other men, women, colleagues, friends, superiors, etc.

SUPPORT GROUPS

For victim partners, especially for women, joining a support group is absolutely essential. Find out from agencies such as the Victim's Assistance Coordinator, from the District Attorney's office, Legal Aid, Department of Human Services, children and family services, and the local community mental health center about the women's support groups in your area.

If there is no support group in your community, suggest to the professionals and the volunteer-social agencies to get the national support group guidelines and form a support group. Counselors alone cannot successfully help a family afflicted with a severe jealousy disorder without a support group and the help from social and humanitarian agencies. They can perhaps help a couple with moderate or reactive jealousy with clinic-based traditional psychotherapy but they cannot provide much benefit in a case of a severe jealousy disorder.

SOCIAL-HUMANITARIAN AGENCIES

Seek help from other agencies, such as the Department of Human Services, Social Security Administration, United Way, legal services, Salvation Army, emergency shelters, children and family services, etc. Find out if you and your children are entitled to any welfare and social security benefits to get you on your feet. Humanitarian clubs, such as the Rotaries, Lions' Club, VFW, Kiwanis club, and the like, may be explored by you, your friends, or an agency in your behalf. Churches in your community may also provide food, clothes, shelter, and cash funds. Department of Human Services may be approached for food stamps, Medicaid eligibility, and other entitlements.

TREATMENT TECHNIQUES

This is not a complete list of treatment techniques for jealousy disorders. However, we have selected a few techniques that we specially recommend to the counselors.

Educate regarding jealousy behavior. Jealousy may be the only way in which a jealous person shows his love. He doesn't know any other way except to assert frequently or, whenever he feels threatened, to assert his claim over the partner, "You are mine. No one else has any right over you." The jealous partner needs to be educated in ways to express his love rather than through the jealousy and to deal with the anxiety about the loss of the partner other than with threats and absolute claims. A nonjealous partner may need reeducation who has learned a wrong lesson from this painful experience and stopped trusting any male friend.

Reframing. A counselor may give a new meaning and frame to a jealous behavior which admittedly has a great nuisance value. The counselor may interpret the jealousy in words to this effect, "By showing jealousy, you are trying to have a closer relationship with your partner and make things better for yourself. What ways other than those of jealousy can you think of to have a better and stronger relationship?"

Identify the self-defeating outcomes of jealousy. A counselor may explain to a jealous person who is extremely dependent on his partner, and clings to her for security, that his jealous behavior has proven to be self-defeating. It may be suggested that if he tries something different rather than just sticking close to her and not allowing anyone else to come near, there is a chance that he might win her love and respect. As in regards to the day to day behavior, he might be advised in these terms, "Sometimes, you should go on your own for an hour or two, meet your friends, go to a restaurant, or a place of your liking, then come and tell her all the exciting things you did." The other partner, who will surely find this as a welcoming relief, may be instructed to appreciate how well the jealous partner has begun to mix and socialize with others.

Seek court-ordered treatment. If a jealous partner has been charged with assault and battery, arrested for public drunkenness, or some other behavior on his part which has brought him to court, the judge may be requested by the counselor, police, or the victim-spouse to order him to receive treatment at the local mental health center or the hospital. A judge may also write a mandatory outpatient treatment order which binds the patient to receive professional treatment. For a jealous person who does not have any motivation for treatment or insight into his jealousy problem, only a legally binding treatment can ensure participation on his part. This will give the counselor some leverage to enforce the jealous partner's attendance in the treatment sessions. This treatment leverage may also be used to promote adherence to behavioral contracts and adoption of nonabusive, nonviolent methods in the transactions at home.

The court ordered treatment is particularly likely to be effective in the case of persons with the delusional disorder of jealousy, as they are generally law abiding people. In many cases, the only crime delusionally disordered persons ever commit is a violent act against their partner.

Role reversal. This may be tried in excessive or morbid jealousy but not delusional jealousy. It must be avoided in a situation in which the jealous partner is highly aggressive and violent. At least initially, it needs to be done in the guidance of a counselor. In role reversal, the nonjealous partner plays the role of the jealous partner. For example, one evening, when the jealous partner comes home from work, the other partner may ask probing questions about who he met and where he spent his time. While asking these persistent questions, she may contrive to display an attitude of suspicion and jealousy. The nonjealous partner may then "fuss" about anyone he socially meets. She may then urge and plead with him not to go out of her sight. Poison kills poison; an overdose of jealousy from the nonjealous partner may shock him out of his jealousy problem. However, be careful that the act does not become real you--that you don't end up as a jealous person yourself.

Role reversal should be tried under the guidance of a counselor who should advise this technique only if the jealous partner believes that the nonjealous partner is not interested in him or believes that he is so dull and boring that the nonjealous partner could hardly be bothered about his staying or leaving. This technique is likely to be more effective when carried out outside the awareness of the jealous partner for its maximum emotional impact. A counselor should work with the couple closely while the role reversal is enacted. A counselor can also use the jealous partner's frustration over the contrived fuss raised by the non-jealous partner. Empathy and understanding of each other can be enhanced by the counselor's interpretations of the couple's feelings and reactions to this artificially created jealousy. Once, symptomatic relief is achieved, the counselor can share information with the jealous partner regarding the technique and its purpose.

This technique is to be used only if both partners are in therapy and if a counselor feels that a jealous partner can tolerate questioning. Counselors are also advised to assure themselves that a jealous person is showing signs of relenting in the power play and domination. For instance, a counselor may ask the jealous partner to share the financial control and decisions with the nonjealous partner and wait to see that progress has been demonstrated in that area. Again, it is recommended in cases of a nondelusional jealousy disorder, provided violent and aggressive behavior is absent.

Confront the jealous partner regarding the controlling behavior. A counselor may decide to directly assault the controlling behavior if such a behavior is not a part of his basic personality. A jealous person needs to learn about the futility of the controlling and restricting behavior. Such behavior is aggressive and characterizes domination of one person's will over another. He should be told in a straightforward manner, "Set her free. You cannot get true love from a slave and you can't get it by incarcerating a person you love. Set her free and she may love you even more." This approach is not likely to work with someone who is characteristically an aggressive and unconscionable person.

SELF-HELP AND SELF-GROWTH TECHNIQUES

Restore and develop your self-esteem. Both partners need to develop their self esteem in areas that are important to them. For example, if you think that you are unattractive or no body really likes you, then you should develop a strong feeling within yourself that you are attractive and you are likeable. If you think you don't know how to act, or whatever you do, causes more problems at home, you must convince yourself that your actions are okay. You need to reassure yourself that you are not the cause of the problem. Go for exercises, groups for image building, socialization, and education. Give positive and reassuring subliminal messages to yourself. Do whatever you think is necessary to raise your self-esteem. If your partner thinks that he is not smart or interesting enough for you, or he thinks that you don't want him around, assure him of his value and interest for you. Tell him objectively of his good points and negative points and what you like about him. Both the partners can help each other and benefit from positive feedback.

Take time just for both of you. If you are not spending much time with each other, take some time just for both of you. Talk to each other about what is on your mind and how you are relating to each other and what you want from each other. If need be, set up a specific time for practicing good communication; call it "communication time," if you will.

Have honest and open communication at all times. Do not give inaccurate facts or lies as those would only confirm the partner's suspicions. For example, if you were attracted by the waitress in the restaurant, do not tell your partner, just to keep peace at home, "No! I didn't even look at her." This would strengthen the distrust and jealousy even more. It would be better to say, "Yes! I did find her attractive." If you were talking to a particular person and your partner asks you, if you talked to so and so, tell him that you did. Denying something that is true, ruins your credibility.

Some victim-partners have nothing to hide but they are afraid of admitting even a peripheral social contact because they think that such an admission would make the partner's jealousy worse. Suppose, your partner knows about that contact, then your denial proves you a liar in the eyes of your partner. Decide which one would be worse.

Do not volunteer information of past sexual affairs. Many partners volunteer information about their past sexual conduct when they were teenagers, affairs they had in a previous marriage or premarital affairs. They do this in the hope that these disclosures would build new trust and confidence in their jealous partner. Sorry, this does not build any more trust. It provides more fuel to the fire.

Draw a distinction between reality and fantasy. If you become jealous because your partner fantasized about someone else, play it down in your mind. Fantasy is not reality. Just remember that if you fantasized about making love with another person, that doesn't mean you actually made love with that person.

Do not corrupt your fantasy. For example, if you fantasize over and over again that your partner is making love with another person or you and another person together are making love with your partner, you have a counter-productive fantasy; it will make your jealousy worse. Be aware that such fantasies torture and provide pleasure at the same time. Whenever, such a fantasy forces itself upon your mind, assert yourself by saying, " No! This does not turn me on," and flash on your mind, a healthy fantasy of you and your partner having a good time and enjoying each other's company.

Do not fantasize about the rival. Each fantasy strengthens the habit of ruminating about the rival, and then you may end up just ruminating about the rival all day long. Instead, concentrate on something you want to achieve for yourself and for others.

Differentiate social interest from sexual interest. Frequently remind yourself that there is a distinction between a reasonable interest in another human being and a sexual attraction for a lover. If a person is interested in another person as a friend or as a colleague, it does not mean that he or she is doing so in order to jump into bed with that individual.

Forget the past and concentrate on the present. Do not waste your time in investigating the affairs of the past. Concentrate on the present. Sit down together with your partner and mutually set the rules for the present behavior at home and outside. Remember that the rules are for both partners and not meant for just one of you to follow.

Do not confess about the past to get rid of your guilt. It might turn an already jealous partner into a pathologically jealous one. Instead, you may want to do something else to assuage your guilt. Do some good deeds for your partner, out of love--not guilt.

Stop rewarding jealous behavior. For example, if every time your partner expresses jealousy regarding your talking to the neighbors or friends and you respond to it by expressing all your love, giving maximum attention and doing the sweetest favors, you are encouraging your partner, "Be jealous and reap the rewards." Also, if jealousy is used in foreplay or for sexual stimulation, the couple should stop that practice.

One partner should not assert his will over the other. Both partners should follow the rule of mutual consent. In particular, you should have intercourse only when both of you consent for it. If you, as a couple, are in counseling, it would be of help to tell your counselor of this behavior and the latter may prescribe sexual intercourse **only** when both of you, as partners, give your explicit consent. Be aware that a domineering jealous partner exploits the emotional and sexual needs of the nonjealous partner. He controls and dictates his wishes by withholding or showering affection and sexual expression. The unspoken message is, "Do as I say and I will love you."

Do not try to solve a jealousy problem with more sex. A jealous partner may become oversexed, sometimes, in an effort to "win over" the partner from the imagined rivals. The nonjealous partner may try to passify and reassure him by initiating sex more frequently. Such attempts can reach a pathetic extreme. You as a couple will be better off by agreeing to go back to your pre-jealousy frequency of sexual intercourse. If you are in therapy, tell your therapist about the inappropriate use of sex in your relationship. He can instruct both of you in how to regulate sex.

Another inappropriate use of sex is frequently reported by the partners of aggressive and domineering jealousy disordered patients. They have to have a major fight before sex. They use sex to dominate and degrade the other partner. For them, a woman becomes an object rather than a person. They want sex at their terms and only when they want it. The partner can never say "No" when the jealousy disordered person wants sex. And if the nonjealous person ever initiated sex, she was seen as a "nympho." If this is happening in your relationship, inform your counselor who may help to modify the inappropriate use of sex through education and assaulting the sexual myths.

Deal directly with the sexual problems and difficulties. Have open and frank discussion of sexual difficulties with a counselor. It is highly likely that sexual dysfunction may be involved with insane jealousy. Problems such as impotence, premature ejaculation, and frigidity need to be treated in a matter of fact way. In many cases, anxiety is the main factor that interferes with sexual performance. Consult a counselor to get a handle on such an anxiety.

Deal directly with the behavioral problem. Consult a marital counselor to address the problems that are interfering with your love and liking for your partner, such as his or her rudeness, selfishness, excessive control, violence, and the like.

Additionally, a counselor may educate you regarding the methods of spying, violence, and control employed in the jealousy disorders. Identify all such methods which are present in your relationship. Help your counselor to draw a specific behavioral contract to reduce such jealousy behaviors.

Clarify the myths and false beliefs you may be carrying about marital loyalty and faithfulness. You may be misinterpreting an act of self-assertion, a difference of opinion, or a step towards individuality, on the part of your partner, as an act of unfaithfulness. Also, the idea of absolute faithfulness, by and large, is untenable. It is not a bad idea to increase your tolerance for the thought that your partner may be unfaithful. Some of you may benefit by a "shock treatment" about the prevalence of extra-marital sex in our society.

Cut down on jealousy provoking behavior. If you are jealous and suspicious and you ask too many questions, you make it impossible for the other partner to give each and every sordid detail. Everyone cannot relate from their memory as well as one would reproduce a scene with a video camera. At the same time, the victim-partner should not try to circumvent the problem by giving vague or short answers. If the questions are upsetting you, it is better to say so, than to suffer silently and give half-hearted, fragmented answers, in a manner that arouses more suspicion.

Develop mutual understanding. Act on the principle that sexual issues are not the only thing in the relationship between the two partners. Each one of you should say to yourself, "I want to learn more about my partner as a person." At a pre-agreed time, you should try a guessing game in which each one of you should guess about the other's preferences, reactions, feelings on specific issues, opinions, and the like. If the answer is wrong, your partner may provide the answer and you may go on till the end of the pre-agreed time.

Remind yourself of the benefits of trust. If you are the jealous partner, understand that you are in a no win situation.

The harder you try, the more you fail. The more you try to control, the more your partner would want to be free. The more force and violence you use, the stronger would become your fears of losing your love to the rival. The irony is that by trying so hard, you are bound to lose. By trusting and letting go of your fears, there is a chance that you might get your peace of mind and an "evidence" of your partner's love and faithfulness.

Observe self-imposed restrictions. Sometimes, there may be a need for self-imposed restrictions. For example, your close involvement on with a colleague, friend, or relative, may be causing a jealous reaction in your partner. Putting that external relationship on hold may not provide a permanent solution, and it will not mollify delusional jealousy but it may provide temporary relief in the case of a partner who is suffering with morbid jealousy or a reactive jealousy. Such temporary relief can be used for initiating treatment and other kinds of help. However, be careful not to let this isolate you from your own support system of friends and relatives. It is most important that you keep your support system active and involved. Any self-imposed restrictions have to be temporary and are effective only when the jealousy disorder is moderate or nondelusional.

Communicate at a designated time. You, as a couple, may also benefit from a "Question & Answer Hour" which is a pre-arranged, pre-agreed, specifically designated time in which the jealous partner is encouraged to ask questions and the victim partner is instructed to flood him with information of even the most trivial details. Both of you may take turns in asking questions. However, you may first practice in the presence of a counselor who may intervene and stop it if it does not bring about a paradoxical effect. A paradoxical effect is present when doing more of the same reduces the problem behavior. For instance, by giving the permission to ask questions and flooding the person with details, it may reduce the jealous questioning. It is expected that in some negative and oppositional subjects this kind of permission to ask question may destroy the motive of power seeking in a couple's interaction. Such a flooding of details may saturate the jealous partner and he may lose interest, as he is not aggressively seeking and demanding the answers. It is most important that it is first done under the guidance of a counselor which would also mean that someone else, not the jealous partner, is the controlling authority.

Try "let's pretend." If you are a nonjealous partner, you may urge your partner to play the pretense game. You may tell your jealous partner, something along these lines, "Pretend that you are not jealous anymore. You should act very confident and self-assured for the next few minutes. Imagine and actually feel that you have nothing to worry about with me or any third person. Whatever I do, you think of a good purpose for it and you keep on feeling good about yourself." If the jealous partner does good in the pretense game, then you should amply reward him or her with love and appreciation. If there is a problem in motivating the jealous partner to participate in this game, then you may make a provision for him or her to ask questions at the end of the game for the same length of time for which the pretense was played.

MEDICATION

Medication can be of very great value in cases of delusional jealousy. A psychiatrist will first determine if the delusional jealousy is a symptom of a more pervasive psychotic illness or if it is a case of a delusional disorder in which delusional jealousy is the primary problem. Antipsychotic drugs are administered in cases of a more pervasive psychotic illness. Antipsychotic medication controls delusions and hallucinations which are the major problems of a psychotic illness. If insane jealousy is part of a mood disorder, then Lithium Carbonate, a mood stabilizer, is administered to treat the manic-depressive (bipolar) disorder. If depression is basically responsible for jealousy with or without other persecutory feelings, antidepressants may be prescribed by your physician. At times, there may be a need to prescribe the antipsychotics and antidepressants together when significant depression is present along with hallucinations and delusions. In some cases, the anxiety accompanying jealousy may be extremely high which may render psychotherapeutic work nearly impossible in the treatment of a jealous partner. Anxiolytics, the medication to reduce anxiety, may be considered by your doctor.

Impotence is frequently reported in patients suffering with male jealousy disorder. Impotence needs to be evaluated for physical or psychological reasons. Good results can be expected from medication and psychological therapies in the treatment of a jealousy disorder which is complicated by male impotence.

One of the nagging problems with jealousy disordered patients is medication compliance. Delusionally jealous patients refuse to receive any treatment including drug therapy because they are convinced that the root of the problem is the erring partner. "If she does not sexually misbehave, I have no problem," is his argument. A morbidly jealous patient fluctuates in his belief regarding the unfaithfulness, so his medication compliance depends on the status of his belief.

The side effects of the medication, too, present a problem. As you are aware antipsychotic drugs can have strong side effects. Patients who are not very motivated for treatment and do not have insight into their problem are not very willing to put up with the side effects of such medication.

As mentioned earlier, organic disorders can also produce a jealousy disorder. Delusion of infidelity is usually prominent in certain kinds of brain disorders. Moreover, the delusions may not be transient; usually they come to stay with the organic disorder. However, the antipsychotic medication may be used with good results to modify the delusion of infidelity.

What is the medical treatment for someone who only has a delusional disorder of jealousy and no other mental disorder? This is a situation in which a delusion of infidelity is firmly entrenched and no other major illness seems to be responsible for delusional jealousy. A delusional disorder is almost impossible to treat by psychotherapy alone. Therefore, a combination of medication and therapy is highly advisable. In the medical literature, studies from Canada report success with Pimozide in cases of delusional disorder of jealousy type. The trade name of Pimozide in the United States is Orap. It seems that Canada is ahead of the U.S. in the medical treatment of this delusional disorder. While promising reports of treatment with this drug are coming from Canada, Pimozide is still an experimental drug in the U.S. Since the professional liability risk is higher with an experimental drug, not many psychiatrists would feel comfortable with administering the drug. We hope Pimozide soon achieves the status of a regular drug.

Last, but not the least, the need for antidepressants and anxiolytics may emerge after the jealousy is modified. Depression or anxiety, or both, which were buried under the jealousy, may appear full force after the jealous rages have been controlled. On the whole, once the jealousy is successfully treated, it is not too uncommon for a variety of other emotional disorders to surface on the scene. Medication for problems, such as depression, anxiety, phobia, or psychotic features may be in order.

In some cases, the victim-partner, too, may need medication for anxiety or depression to cope with the situation.

HOSPITALIZATION

In cases where outpatient treatment fails, or the jealous patient refuses to get professional help, and the risk of violence seems substantial, hospital admission is definitely indicated for the safety of the patient and his partner. If a person with delusional jealousy has demonstrated jealousy-related violence towards the partner, dangerous consequences may occur if the condition is left untreated. The stories related in this book reveal that in the worst scenario, homicide or suicide is a possible outcome.

The question arises how does one make a person accept hospitalization if he is not even willing to take treatment at the outpatient level? Well! You may have to gather all the support you can find: a trusted and respected friend, or relative of the jealous partner; the family doctor; resources from the clinic and the court system, etc. A delusionally jealous person who is afraid to let the partner out of his sight, may find the proposal of hospital treatment rather terrifying, as it involves his absence from home. He is afraid of what all she might do in his absence. He might think, "This is all her plan. She wants to put me away in the hospital so she can run around with other men." Many delusionally jealous patients leave against medical advice or elope from the hospital so that they can rush home and watch their partners.

Some insanely jealous patients, while in the hospital, may become evasive and reticent in talking about their delusions of infidelity. They may also claim recovery from their delusions of infidelity for the benefit of the physician, knowing fully well that only a feigned recovery can bring about discharge from the hospital. The treatment team at the hospital should carefully examine such self-reports of recovery and compare it with the reports from the family members. Prior to a discharge from the hospital, the patient may be sent home on a couple of "home passes," preferably overnight, to spend time with his family. The staff should obtain confidential reports, separately, from the various family members to ascertain if jealousy is still causing problems at home.

Hospital staff may have to face the brunt of his ire as he may blame the hospital for not making his wife admit of her acts of adultery, or for siding with his wife against him. He may be furious with the staff for keeping him in the hospital "while his house is on fire." He may suspect that the doctor or a member of the staff has formed a secret liaison with his partner. He may develop jealous rage or fear in response to this triangle.

To sell the idea of hospitalization to a jealousy disordered partner, the victim-spouse may need to involve other family members and relatives who, hopefully, can exercise influence over the jealous partner. She may also need to discuss it with the family doctor and together make a concerted effort to persuade the patient to seek hospitalization. If all else fails, obtain a **commitment order** for emergency treatment and evaluation through psychiatric hospitalization. Such a commitment order says that the person in question is dangerous to himself or to others and is not willing to receive treatment, or is not competent to make a meaningful decision with regard to the treatment for his or her mental condition.

A commitment order is typically signed by two physicians but some states allow one physician and one licensed clinical psychologist to authorize commitment. In practice, one of the two signing physicians could be the admitting doctor at the hospital. In that case, the family may need to contact only one physician or a psychologist (if that state allows it) to agree for signing the commitment order and the physician at the hospital may endorse it to make it legal. Each State has its own laws for legal commitment to a psychiatric hospital; the local community mental health center or the emergency room of the local hospital may be consulted for advice on the commitment orders. If you are already consulting mental health professionals, approach them for their opinion regarding involuntary treatment on a commitment order.

If a jealousy disorder is so severe as to require hospitalization, then the most effective form of hospitalization may be if both the partners were admitted to the hospital together to be treated as a couple. If a unit in the hospital is run as a "couple unit" approximating the home condition, it may be easier to target some day-to-day concrete problems of the marital relationships and effect desirable changes.

SEPARATION AND DIVORCE

A woman thinks that if she fails her family, she is a total failure; She wants to keep the family together even though she pays a very high price for it. In a few cases, when jealousy gets out of hand and a woman is subjected to severe violence, she moves out of the house. It is a very big step, a very courageous step on the part of the female partner. If she has young children, it is even more difficult. If she has familial and social support and has some resources to fall back on, it becomes a little easier for her than for someone who has none.

However, a separation from a jealous partner typically lasts just a few weeks. The jealous partner changes his behavior drastically when faced with a separation. He cries, pleads, and begs her for forgiveness. He professes his love, renders most vehement apologies, and makes wonderful promises and vows for peace if she would only come back. If that doesn't work, then the jealous partner, who has an aggressive and domineering personality, uses threat of harm and violence. He tries to prevent her from having access to money, house, or car, as all such things can make her independent of him. He tries to and often succeeds in convincing her that his jealous rage and possessive control of her was a result of his absolute love. When she returns, there may be a second honeymoon for a while before the jealousy gets the better of him.

A separation can be helpful if the non-jealous spouse uses it to negotiate terms for the future behavior. But first, she needs to make up her mind, whether she wants to improve their relationship or get out of it. If she wants a divorce, she should consult a lawyer. If she wants improvement in their relationship, she should consult a mental health professional. The jealous partner must start receiving treatment before the couple is reunited. In fact, it is best if the couple reunites after some progress is actually made in treatment. A jealous partner has to demonstrate his motivation and his will to change by carrying out the assignments and fulfilling the behavioral contracts proposed in the treatment.

There comes a time when a victim-partner must resolve for divorce. Safety must come first. In view of an ongoing danger from the jealous partner, divorce may be the only option she has. If she senses the situation is dangerous for her, she doesn't feel safe in living with her partner, or she has tried everything else and not seen much relief in the jealousy disorder, she has to get out. As it is pointed out by experts, in intractable forms of delusional jealousy, the only effective treatment is the "geographical treatment." The couple must live apart from each other.

In our experience, many women would have divorced their jealous and violent partners a long time ago if they had the wherewithal to do it. Some women do not have the education or the work skills to become independent and support their children. Some have been nudged into a dependent, confined, and isolated existence, so the idea of separating and grappling with life on their own seems most frightening to them.

According to our observations, among the women married to jealous partners, even the ones who have been working for several years, do not have a bank account or a credit card in their own name. They have no credit history with any credit bureau. They have no property in their name. They cannot apply and get any credit in their name. On top of that, many women are afraid for their life if their partner is jealous and violent. Many possessive and controlling men, if their partner tries to become independent, will mess up her car, get her utilities cut off, and batter and harass her in dozens of different ways.

A woman who takes the daring step of moving out needs considerable social and financial support. Free children and family services, legal services, baby sitting, health services, food stamps, temporary shelter, and the similar other practical services may make it possible for a woman to get out and stay away from a violent and oppressive man.

Some women may need help to readjust and affiliate with other men. After a painful relationship such as the one with a jealous person, it may be difficult for them to trust any man.

On the other hand, we have seen people who had gotten out of a relationship with a jealous partner and got into another one with a similar problem. A nonjealous partner needs to examine the question, "What is it in the jealous person's courting behavior that attracts me so profoundly?" A person who is capable of intense jealousy may be extraordinarily passionate and demonstrative, which may mask his possessiveness and need for control. Also, he can manage to hide his jealousy, as he is still busy in bonding and intensifying the bonding. However, for a person who has just experienced the full range of this emotion, it may not be difficult to identify the pattern.

CHILDREN OF A JEALOUS PARENT

Children of a family where one of the parent is jealous are most likely to be deprived. The jealous father may resent them or doubt their paternity and the nonjealous mother may be afraid of showing her affection to them. As a jealous father is likely to be emotionally underdeveloped and may not have developed the nurturant and protective parental behaviors, he may relate to his children as a peer or a rival rather than as a parent. He may not be truly focussed on the children to respond to their emotional needs. His partner is the only and primary object for him to protect, and he may be too preoccupied with monitoring and controlling her.

Children of a jealous parent feel terribly insecure and have an uneasy feeling about the tense situation, but they don't know what to make out of it. A nonjealous parent doesn't tell children what is going on because she wants to protect them. They may overhear accusations regarding unfaithfulness, allegations regarding true paternity, arguments, and crying. They may witness inexplicable rage and sadness but learn to ignore it.

The question for children of an insanely jealous parent, "Will I also become jealous like Dad (or Mom)?" is critical. Many children of a jealous parent live under this fear. These fears are revived whenever they experience jealousy, even a normal jealousy. They panic, thinking, "That's it. It has gotten me." We need to assure them by teaching them about normal jealousy, or, better, by teaching them about healthy jealousy. Children of a jealous parent need to be reassured that there is no evidence that morbid or delusional jealousy is hereditary. However, some jealousy that they see in themselves may have been learned while growing up in a family with an insanely jealous parent. It may be reassuring to know that such jealousy behaviors can be easily unlearned by self-education and therapy.

SIGNS OF A FAVORABLE OUTCOME

A partner who is insanely jealous has a good chance of recovery or relief from the problem if he has one or more of the following:

1. If the outbreak of jealousy occurs after forty years of age.
2. If there is no outbreak of jealousy for the first two or three years of the marriage life.
3. No hallucinations, that is, the jealous partner does not **hear** or **see** things which are not really there.
4. No pseudomemories, that is, the jealous person does not **"remember"** events that did not really take place.
5. Absence of the delusion of infidelity. In other words, performance of daily routines and trivia is not the only evidence he provides of her unfaithfulness. He has at least seen her talking with another person which he misinterprets as the "goings on."
6. Moderate to severe depression.
7. Little or no history of violence.
8. Absence of law and order problems, such as arrests, convictions, criminal and other antisocial behaviors.
9. Evidence of tendering apologies or expressing regrets for accusatory and other jealous behaviors.

10. History of an acute jealous reaction or of a sudden outbreak of jealousy as opposed to a gradual worsening of jealousy.

11. During childhood, there is absence of severe conditions, such as a broken home, family violence, parental neglect, and severe physical or sexual abuse.

A COMMENT

Jealousy is a primal emotion. It is a feature of the animal world and the human society. It exists at the instinctual as well as the emotional-psychological level. If there is a strong intimate emotional bonding between two people, there is bound to be jealousy. By its very nature, intimacy requires exclusion of a third person from a relationship which is very private and personal.

However, as we mature, we learn to tolerate and share this intimate twosome relationship with a third person. A couple shares it with their child. A child learns to share his mother with the father and the siblings. To become emotionally mature means learning to handle one's jealousy, be able to laugh at it, and allow our partner the freedom to relate to others.

Perhaps with the emphasis on "sexual freedom," beginning in the 60s, we led ourselves to think that we have ridden ourselves of sexual jealousy. The flower children were expected to make love and not war. Premarital sex, extra-marital affair, divorce and remarriage came to be seen as part of the modern society. The grown-ups of the blended families are sure to have overcome their primitive feelings of sexual jealousy. That we know is a wishful thinking. In reality, there are many people out there who are jealous like the wounded animals. The privacy and secrecy of the modern couples shroud their jealousy. Most couples move away from their extended families and friends. They live in faceless and nameless urban areas. Friends and relatives hesitate to invade the couple's privacy. No one knows how many individuals are keeping their partners restricted and chained in the privacy of their homes because they are scared of losing them to someone else.

Insane jealousy is fear. It is poor self esteem. Above all, it is a drive for power and control by one person over the other. It is an act of aggression and domination by us of someone we claim to love. Except in the severe degrees of a jealousy disorder, an act of abuse and violence on someone else or on our own self is a voluntary act. We let it get out of hand. We are responsible for such a behavior and we can exercise control over it.

In a mature loving relationship, there is no room for domination of one will over the other. In such a relationship, the two persons feel dependent on each other. Both respect each other and treat each other as equals. Both feel adequate and competent in their own right. And regardless of the consequences, both trust and allow each other the freedom to grow and pursue their interests and ambitions. Then they come to be truly emotionally bonded to each other.

Let us not be afraid of being betrayed and hurt. Even if we do get betrayed and hurt, we will still be paying much less a price than we would if we were to continually live in distrust and fear.

JEALOUSY BIBLIOGRAPHY

The bibliography of jealousy and related disorders is in two sections. The first section is the "References" which is an alphabetical listing of all the references cited in the manual. The second section, "Suggested Reading," is subdivided in two parts: "Jealousy in Literary Works" and "Jealousy in Psychological Works."

REFERENCES

American Psychiatric Association (1987): Diagnostic and Statistical Manual of Mental Disorders, Third Edition, Revised (DSM-III-R). Washington D.C. American Psychiatric Association

Chaucer, Geoffrey (1987) Canterbury Tales. in the Great Books of the Western World, Vol.22, (ed) The University of Chicago, Encyclopedia Britannica, Inc., Twenty-Ninth Printing. pp.318-338

Grillet, Alain Robbe (1957) La Jalousie

Shakespeare, William (1987) Othello, the Moore of Venice in the Great Books of the Western World, Vol.2, (eds) The University of Chicago, Encyclopedia Britannica, Inc., Twenty-Ninth Printing, P.229

Old Testament (1973) in New American Standard Bible, Reference Edition, Collins World, The Lockman Foundation, La Habra, California

SUGGESTED READING

JEALOUSY IN LITERARY WORKS

Boccacio. Ninth Novel of the Second Day.

Capellanus, A. The Art of Courtly Love. New York: Frederick Ungar, 1957

Tolstoy, Leo. The Kreutzer Sonata, translated by Isai Kamen New York: Random House, 1957

JEALOUSY IN PSYCHOLOGICAL WORKS

Adams, V.(1980). Getting at the Heart of Jealousy. Psychology Today, 13(2), 38-47, 102, 105-106.

Barag, G.(1949.) A Case of Pathological Jealousy. Psychoanalytic Quarterly 18: 1- 18.

Bergler, E. (1956) Unconscious Reasons for 'Husbands' Confessions' to Their Jealous Wives, Psychiatric Quarterly. 30:73-76.

Bringle, R. G. & Evenbeck, S., (1979). A Study of Jealousy as a Dispositional Characteristic. Ina M. Cook & A. Wilson (Eds.) Love and Attraction 201-204. New York: Pergamon Press.

Brunswick, R. M. (1929). The Analysis of a Case of Paranoia (delusion of jealousy). Journal of Nervous and Mental Disease 70: 5-21, 155- 178.

Buunk, B. (1981). Jealousy in Sexually Open Marriages. Alternative Life Styles 4, 357- 372.

Buunk, B. (1986) Husband's Jealousy. In R.A. Lewis & R.E. Salt (eds.) Men in Families 97-114, Beverly Hills, CA, Sage Publications.

Cobb, J. (1979). Morbid Jealousy. British Journal of Hospital Medicine, 21, 511-518.

Coen, S.J. (1987). Pathological Jealousy. International Journal of Psycho-analysis, 68: 99-108.

Constantine, L. A. (1976). Jealousy from Theory to Intervention, in D. Olsen (ed.) Treating Relationships, 383-398 Lake Mills, IA, Graphic.

Davis, K. (1936). Jealousy and Sexual Property, Social Forces, 14, 395-405.

Docherty, J. P., and Ellis, J. (1976) A New Concept and Finding in Morbid Jealousy, American Journal of Psychiatry, 133: 679-683.

Farber, L.H.(1973). On jealousy. Commentary, 56 (4), 58-65.

Feldman, A. B. (1952). Othello's Obsessions. American Imago, 9: 147-64.

Fenichel, O. (1935). A Contribution to the Psychology of Jealousy. In The Collected Papers of Otto Fenichel. First Series, New York: Norton, 1953, pp.349-62.

Gessel, A. (1906). "Jealousy," American Journal of Psychology 17, 437-496.

Jones, E. (1961). Jealousy. In Papers on Psychoanalysis, 325-340, Boston:Beacon.

Klein. M. (1951). Envy and Gratitude Tavistock Publications, Ltd.

Langfeldt, G. (1961). The Erotic Jealousy Syndrome. Acta Scandinavia Supplementum 151, 36.

Lewis, A.J. (1938). "Alcoholic Psychoses" British Encyclopedia of Medical Practice 8, 322.

Lovel, Barnes, J.F. (1954). "Marriage, Paranoia, and Paranoid States, "Med. Press., 232.

Mace, D.R.(1962). Two Faces of Jealousy. Mccall, 89(8), 56.

Mathes, E.W. & Severa, N. (1981). Jealousy, Romantic Love, and Liking: Theoretical Considerations and Preliminary Scale Development. Psychological Reports, 23-31, 49.

Mathes, E.W., Rooter, P.M. & Jeorger, M. (1982). A Convergent Validity Scale Study of Six Jealousy Scales. Psychological Reports, 50, 1143-1147.

Mathes, E.W., Phillips, J.T., Skowron, J. & Dick, W. E. (1982). Behavioral Correlates of the Interpersonal Jealousy

Scale. Educational and Psychological Measurement, 42, 1227-1231.

Mathes, E.W. et al. (1985). Jealousy: Loss of Relationship Rewards, Loss of Self- esteem, Depression, Anxiety and Anger. Journal of Personality and Social Psychology, 48: 1552-1561.

May, R. (1972) Love, Jealousy and Innocence. Mccall, 100 (2), 83, 122-126.

Mooney, J.B. (1965). Pathologic Jealousy and Psychochemotherapy. British Journal of Psychiatry, III, 1023-1042.

Mowatt, R.R. (1966). Morbid Jealousy and Murder. Tavistock Publications, London, 1966.

Munro, A. (1984). Excellent Response of Pathologic Jealousy to Pimozide. Canadian Medical Assocation Journal, 131,852-853.

O'Neil, W. (1898). "A Case of Jealousy," Lancet, 1898, i, 223.

Pao, P.N. (1969). Pathological Jealousy, Psychoanalytic Quarterly 38: 616-638.

Price, John. (1976). Phedon's Fury: Some Psychoanalytic Notes on the Faerie Queene II, Canto IV., J. of Literature and Psychology, Vol. 26 (4) 167-173.

Retterstol, N. (1966). Paranoid and Paranoiae Psychoses. Universited for Lapet, Oslo, Bergen, Thomas, Springfield.

Riviere. J. (1932). Jealousy as a Mechanism of Defence. International Journal of Psycho-analysis, 13, 414-424.

Schmideberg, M. (1953) Some Aspects of Jealousy and of Feeling Hurt, Psychoanal. Rev. [1953] 40:1-16

Scott, P.D. (1977). British Journal of Psychiatry. 131, 127.

Seeman, M.V. (1979). Pathological Jealousy. Psychiatry, 42: 351-361.

Seidenberg, R. (1952). Jealousy: The Wash. Psychoanalytic Review, 39:345-353.

Semelaigne, R. (1902). Delusions Resulting from Jealousy, Journal of Mental Science, 48, 131.

Shepherd, M. (1961). Morbid Jealousy. Journal of Mental Science, 107, 687-753.

Smith, G. (1959). Iago the Paranoiac. American Imago, 16:155-167.

Speilman, P.M. (1971). Envy and Jealousy: An Attempt at Clarification. Psychoanalytic Quarterly, 40: 4,59,82.

Stefanowski, D. (1893). Morbid Jealousy, Alienist and Neurologist, St. Louis, 14, 375.

Stoller, R. J. Sexual Excitement, Archives of General Psychiatry (1976) 33: 899-909

Teisman, M.W. (1970). Jealousy: Systemic Problem-Solving Therapy with Couples, Family Process, 18: 151-160.

Tiggelaar, J.I. (1956). Pathologic Jealousy and Jealous Delusions, Folio of Psychiatry and Neurology, 59,522.

Todd, J. & Dewhurst, K. (1955). The Othello Syndrome. A Study in the Psychopathology of Sexual Jealousy. Journal of Nervous and Mental Disease, 122, 367-374.

Turbott, John (1981). Morbid Jealousy: An Unusual Presentation with the Reciprocal Appearance of Psychopathology in Either Spouse. Australian & New Zealand Journal of Psychiatry, 15(2), 164-167.

GLOSSARY

AMOROUS JEALOUSY: See SEXUAL JEALOUSY.

CONJUGAL PARANOIA: A term used earlier in the psychiatric literature to describe the condition in which one partner is morbidly or delusionally jealous of the other partner. Conjugal paranoia is also known as the OTHELLO COMPLEX.

DELUSION: A false belief which is fixed and unshakeable. A delusional patient does not give up his delusion even when confronted with logical reasoning or facts.

DELUSIONAL JEALOUSY: When a person is convinced without a due cause that his or her partner is unfaithful.

DELUSION OF JEALOUSY: "Delusion of jealousy" is referred to in the earlier psychiatric literature but it is really a misnomer. Jealousy is real--it is not a delusion. See DELUSION OF INFIDELITY.

DELUSION OF INFIDELITY: A conviction without a due cause that one's partner is unfaithful. The term "delusion of infidelity" is preferred to "delusion of jealousy" because accusations of infidelity are obvious while certain components of jealousy may be subtle and can only be inferred, not directly observed.

DELUSIONAL DISORDER, JEALOUS TYPE: A disorder in which a person has a delusion of infidelity as the primary disorder and there is no other mental disorder, brain abnormality or chemical condition associated with such a delusion.

DISORDERS OF JEALOUSY: When sexual jealousy is irrational, excessive, unfounded or disproportionate to the threat of losing one's lover to a rival. The rival may be a real or imaginary person, specific or a nonspecific person. There are three noted disorders of jealousy: "morbid jealousy," "delusional jealousy," and "delusional disorder, jealous type." Colloquially, it is referred to as INSANE JEALOUSY. In a jealousy disorder, the problem lies in the individual while in normal jealousy, the problem may be in the partner's relationship.

HALLUCINATIONS: Perception of sensory events which are really not there. Auditory hallucinations and visual hallucinations refer to "hearing voices" or "seeing visions or things" that are really not there.

HEALTHY JEALOUSY: A jealousy is healthy in which the assessment of the threat of loss and self-examination is accurate, the equality and freedom of the other partner is respected, and both partners are enriched and strengthened by it. Note that normal jealousy is not always healthy or rational.

INSANE JEALOUSY: See DISORDERS OF JEALOUSY.

JEALOUSY: A feeling of pain, fear, anger and other related negative emotions arising from the real or threatened loss of a "prized possession" to a rival.

LOVER'S JEALOUSY: See SEXUAL JEALOUSY.

MORBID JEALOUSY: Excessive and irrational fear that one's partner is unfaithful--a jealousy disorder without the delusion of infidelity.

NORMAL JEALOUSY: A feeling of pain, fear, anger, and other negative emotions directly in proportion to the actual or threatened loss to the rival. If it is a "normal" jealousy, it indicates that other people too would experience jealousy in equal measures under similar circumstances. In a normal jealousy, the problem may be in the relationship between the two partners, but in a jealousy disorder, the problem is within the individual. However, a normal jealousy is not necessarily a rational jealousy. See RATIONAL JEALOUSY.

OTHELLO COMPLEX Another term for CONJUGAL PARANOIA (morbid or delusional jealousy) based on Shakespeare's play Othello in which Othello became obsessed with the "infidelity" of his wife, Desdemona.

PATHOLOGICAL JEALOUSY: A term used for the

PROJECTIVE JEALOUSY: A psychoanalytic term to indicate a form of jealousy (or the fear of losing one's partner to a rival). It stems, not from the partner's unfaithfulness, but from the jealous person's own unfaithfulness to his partner.

PSEUDOMEMORY: A false memory of events, that is to "remember" or "recall" something that really did not take place.

RATIONAL JEALOUSY: A jealousy which is characterized by accuracy, self-criticism, and self-control. A rationally jealous person is aware of his feelings of jealousy and can laugh at his own self. He does not let the jealousy reaction get out of hand. He does not become destructive or overreactive. Rational jealousy is healthy. However, normal jealousy is not always rational.

REACTIVE JEALOUSY: A feeling of pain, fear, anger, and other related negative emotions in response to a real loss or real threat of loss of one's lover to a rival, e.g., a person may react jealously after the exposure of his or her partner's extra-marital affair. However, the degree of jealousy may be exaggerated and disproportionate to the actual loss or threat of loss of love which makes it different from realistic jealousy.

REALISTIC JEALOUSY: A feeling of pain, fear, anger, and other related negative emotions in response to a real loss or real threat of loss of one's lover to a rival. However, the jealousy response is proportionate to the threat or the actual loss, as the case may be.

ROMANTIC JEALOUSY: See Sexual Jealousy.

SEXUAL JEALOUSY: Also known as AMOROUS JEALOUSY, LOVER'S JEALOUSY, OR ROMANTIC JEALOUSY. Jealousy is a broad term and used with all types of relationships, friends, colleagues, competitors, peers, etc. Sexual jealousy is the jealousy used only in the sexual context. Thus, it is the feeling of pain, fear (of being supplanted in affection by the partner), anger, and other related negative emotions arising from the real or threatened loss of one's sexual partner to a rival.

JEALOUSY QUOTES

But jealous souls will not be answer'd so;
They are not ever jealous for the cause,
But jealous for they are jealous. 'Tis a monster
Begot upon itself, born on itself.
    (Othello, III, IV, 160)

A most violent passion it is where it taketh place, an
unspeakable torment, a hellish torture, an internal plague,
...a fury, a continual fever full of suspicion, fear and sorrow,
a martyrdom, a mirthmarring monster."
(The Anatomy of Melancholy, Robert Burton, 1621)

Those which are jealous proceed from suspicion to hatred;
from hatred to frenzie; from frenzie to injurie, murder, and
despair.
(The Anatomy of Melancholy, Robert Burton, 1621)

O! beware, my lord of jealousy;
It is the green-eyed monster which doth mock
The meat it feeds on; that cuckold lives in bliss
Who, certain of his fate, loves not his wronger;
But, O! what damned minutes tells he o'er
Who dotes, yet doubts; suspects, yet soundly loves!
    (Othello, III, iii, 165)

Art is a jealous mistress
(Ralph Waldo Emerson, The Conduct of Life[1860] Wealth)

I will not say with Lord Hale, that "The Law will not admit
of no rival" ...but I will say that it is a jealous mistress, and
requires a long and constant courtship. It is not to be won
by trifling favors, but by lavish homage.
(Joseph Story, The Value and Importance of Legal Studies
[August 5, 1829])

The jealous are the readiest of all to forgive, and all women
know it.
    (Dostoevski. The Brothers Karmazov [18;79-1880]
Book VIII, 3)

The venom clamors of a jealous woman
Poison more deadly than a mad dog's tooth.
(Shakespeare, The Comedy of Errors, V, i, 69)

Jealousy is always born together with love, but it does not
always die when love dies.
(Francois, Duc de la Rochefoucauld, 1678, Reflections; or,
Sentences and Moral Maxims. Epigraph, 361)

In jealousy there is more self-love than love
        (Ibid 324)

Jealousy feeds upon suspicion, and it turns into fury or it
ends as soon as we pass from suspicion to certainty.
        (Ibid 32)

The ear of jealousy heareth all things.
(The Apocrypha, the Wisdom of Solomon 1:10)

Nor jealousy Was understood, the injured lover's hell
(Milton, Paradise Lost, 1667, I 449)

Set me as a seal upon thine heart, as a seal upon thine arm:
for love is strong as death; jealousy is cruel as the grave.
    (Song of Solomon, 8:6)

Jealousy is the rage of a man: therefore he will not spare in
the day of vengeance.
(The Proverbs 6:34)

Jealousy the jaundice of the soul
(Dryden, The Hind and the Panther, 1687, l, 73)

This carpenter had lately wed a wife,
Whom he loved better than he loved his life.
And she was come to eighteen years of age,
Jealous he was and held her close in the cage. For she was
wild and young, and he was old,
And deemed himself as like to be cuckold.
(translated by J.G. Nicholson, Chaucer, Miller's Tale in
Canterbury Tales, Great Books of Western World, 22,
P.213)

He wept and he lamented, pitifully;
And therewithal the fire of jealousy
Lest that his wife should fall to some folly,
So burned within the heart that he would fain,
Both him and her some man had swiftly slain.

(Januarie is very possessive and jealous of his wife)

For neither after death nor in his life
Would he that she were other's love or wife,
But dress in black and live in widow's state
Lone as the turtle-dove that's lost her mate

(When Januarie became blind, he became morbidly jealous)

...he could not renounce, as done,
His jealousy, from which he never won.
For this his passion was so outrageous...
That neither in his hall nor other house
Nor any other place, not ever, no,
He suffered her to ride or walking go,
Unless he had his hand on her alway:
(Chaucer, Merchant's Tale, Ibid, p. 332-333)

Among all the passions wherewith human minds are perplexed, there is none that so galleth with restless despite as the infectious sore of jealousy; for all other griefs are either to be appeased with sensible persuasions, to be cured with wholesome counsel, to be relieved in want, or by tract of time to be worn out, jealousy only excepted, which is so sauced with suspicious doubts and pinching mistrust, that whoso seeks by friendly counsel to raze out this hellish passion, it forthwith suspecteth that he giveth this advice to cover his own guiltiness. Yes, whoso is pained with this restless torment doubteth all, distrusteth himself, is always frozen with fear and fired with suspicion, having that wherein consisteth all his joy to be the breeder of his misery.
(Robert Greene, Pandosto, in William Shakespeare, The Winter's Tale, New American Library, 1963, pp. 155-177)

But there is another reason why husband and wife cannot love each other and that is that very substance of love, without which true love cannot exist--I mean jealousy-- is in such a case very much frowned upon and they should avoid it like the pestilence; but lovers should always welcome it as the mother and the nurse of love.
(Andreas Capellanus, the twelfth century author of The Art of courtly Love, New York: Frederick Ungar, 1957, p.17)

The hatred towards an object loved, together with the envy of another is called jealousy
(B. Spinoza, Ethics, London, Dent. 1948, original work published in 1677)

Jealous person is like a scorpion, who out of rage and frustration of jealousy, will sting itself.
(F. Nietzsche, 1880, The Wanderer and his Shadow. In ed. Kaufman [Trans.] Basic writings of Nietzsche, New York, Modern Library, 1966.

Has anyone counted the victims of jealousy?   Daily a revolver cracks somewhere or other because of jealousy; daily a knife finds entrance into a warm body; daily some unhappy ones, racked by jealousy and life, weary, sink into fathomless depths. What are all hideous battles, narrated by history, when compared to this frightful passion jealousy.
(Stekel, W. 1921, The Depths of Soul [S. A. Tannenbaum, Trans.] London, Kegan Paul)

INDEX

Notes

This space is offered to you by the authors to jot down your own thoughts and feelings about the problems of jealousy.

WE WOULD APPRECIATE TO HEAR FROM YOU!

We offer this space for you to share your own thoughts, comments, and experiences with us. Please do take the trouble of writing to us We even begin this letter for you.

Dear Vijai, Ashley, Sabrina, and Holly,

Mail it to: Mind Publications, Inc.
P.O. Box 4254
Cleveland, TN 37320-4254

ORDER FORM

Please send me a copy of the book, INSANE
JEALOUSY.

1 copy only $ 16.95

---copies(#0f copiesX16.00)   -----

Shipping & Handling, first book   2.50

1.00 for each additional book   ----

Air Mail (add another 3.00per book if
 you don't want to wait for the book
 rate mail)   ----

Total amount $----

Please write your check to Mind
Publications Inc for the total amount.

I understand I may return any book for a
full refund of the price of the book if I
am not satisfied.

Please mail this Order Form with your
check to:

Mind Publications, Inc
P.O. Box 4254
Cleveland, TN 37320-4254